More of Everything Else

Saratoga -- Lexington -- Thoroughbred

By

David A. Siegenthaler

Cover and Illustrations
By
W. C. Pope

ISBN   1-891181-00-9

Library of Congress Catalog Card Number: 98-86350

Siegenthaler, David A. 1935 -
  More of Everything Else;
  Saratoga, Lexington, Thoroughbred
  Illustrations by W. C. Pope
  1. Title, 2. History, 3. Horse Racing, 4. Saratoga,
  5. Lexington, 6. Thoroughbred

For Margie

Acknowledgments

From start to finish-with respect to completing this book, I have been supported by many persons and places. To all of them, I extend my grateful appreciation. In particular, my daughters, Ann Sturbin and Julie Loprete; also,

Lexington, KY: Cathy Schenck, Keeneland Association Library. Keeneland Racecourse.

Saratoga Springs, NY: Elinor Riter; Jean Stamm and Ellen DeLalla, Saratoga Springs Public Library; Tom Gilcoyne and his associates, National Museum of Racing and Hall of Fame.

Utica, NY: Kathy Kelly; Cathy Larrabee; Bill Pope; Judy Sweet; Marlene Letner; Rob Jenkins.

I would also like to thank the staff people assigned to room 315, the research area at the New York City Public Library, for their assistance.

David A. Siegenthaler

Table of Contents

Preface

I published a book titled, "A part of Everything Else," in 1996. The book was a human interest story blended with the history of Cape Ann, the peninsula located on the Atlantic, 30 miles northeast of Boston, Massachusetts. The cape was a favorite vacation spot for my family going back to July of 1979.

As my 1996 book proved successful, I felt I owed it to myself and to the people who were nice enough to buy it, to write another one. I searched for something to write about and decided to do another human interest story, once again writing about a subject dear to my heart. The book you are about to read is a human interest story blended with history of Saratoga Springs, New York, Lexington Kentucky, and the "Sport of Kings," Thoroughbred breeding and racing.

My idea for this book dates back to the early 1960's. I worked in Saratoga Springs doing public relations work at the Saratoga Harness Racing Association, the less famous of the two race tracks located at the spa. I later married a girl from Saratoga and returned to my home town, Utica, New York to begin a long career with a local financial institution and raise two daughters. Saratoga was very important to my family, a second home, especially during the summer months. This resort area provided many great experiences for our children. They had as many friends in Saratoga as they did in Utica.

I really got hooked on Saratoga; one of my favorite things to do was to attend the annual yearling sales every August. It was thrilling to watch the "rich and famous" purchase yearlings and horses of racing age. On August 7, 1973 I witnessed the sale of a yearling, bay colt by "What a Pleasure" out of "Fool-Me-Not". The word around the Fasig-Tipton sales paddock that night was, "he toes out" and the horse people turned to other horses due to the obvious defects of the colt listed as hip number 53 in the catalogue.

Leroy Jolley, a young trainer liked the colt and purchased him for $20,000 for John L. Greer of Knoxville, Tennessee. I followed the impressive career of this bargain horse, to be named Foolish Pleasure. Foolish Pleasure emerged as two year old champion in 1974. In 1975, as a three year old he won the Flamingo, Wood Memorial and the first leg of the triple crown, the Kentucky Derby.

In July of 1975 a match race viewed by millions was run between Foolish Pleasure and the three-year old champion filly Ruffian. The contest, considered by many to be an "unnatural" event ended in tragedy. At the halfway point, Ruffian had gained the lead on the colt, when the filly running extremely fast broke a leg. She continued to run for a few strides, then stopped. Foolish Pleasure went on to victory. All efforts to save Ruffian were unsuccessful and she was destroyed.

As happens with many great racehorses, when racing is no longer part of their life, they retire to the breeding farm. Foolish Pleasure was syndicated for $4.5 million in 1975. He sired 37 stakes winners and died in 1994 at the age of 22. The book features the careers of several bargain yearlings that went on to achieve "greatness" in the sport of Thoroughbred racing.

I believe in the old saying, "life is a journey." For sure writing this book was for me a journey. I have met many fine people since I first began to develop my idea back in 1995. My initial conversation was with Terence R. P. Collier, Director of Marketing for Fasig-Tipton Company. He was kind enough to direct me to Ellen Kiser and Ray

Paulick of The Blood-Horse magazine in Lexington, Kentucky. In addition to the interviews that are part of chapters one and four and the individuals listed in the acknowledgment section, there were others that impacted the writing. People that crossed my path during the last two and one half years.

Bill Turner, trainer of Triple Crown winner Seattle Slew, Diana Rice Turnbull, of Woodland Park Bookstore in Lexington, John and Janice DeMarco, Lyrical Ballad Bookstore in Saratoga, and Joe Pope, Manager of Esposito's Tavern, located across from Belmont Park. If you go to Belmont, you have to visit Esposito's. I met with Bill Turner at Barn number 38, Belmont Park on May 14, 1997. During my visit, Bill introduced me to his assistant, Pat Rich and her daughter, Jessica, a student at Colgate University, located near my home in upstate New York.

On that day I also stopped over at Barn 26, which was occupied by LeRoy Jolley, trainer of Foolish Pleasure. Jolley was not at the barn, so I missed talking to the man who won the 1975 Derby with Foolish Pleasure and again in 1980 with Genuine Risk.

My point in mentioning these people is because when writing a book like this, on going conversation plays a major role. I sincerely believe it is the key to making the book "interesting."

In this book, I have expressed my love for the city of Saratoga Springs. For the purpose of the writing, I extend my interest in Saratoga's history to include the history of Lexington. My initial visit to Lexington in October of 1995 was a positive experience, enhanced by four days of research at the Keeneland Association Library located on the Keeneland Racecourse.

I had an opportunity during this trip to discuss my book with Ray Paulick, Editor-in-Chief of The Blood-Horse, a magazine published weekly in Lexington. I decided after talking with Ray, that there is a definite link between these two communities, despite some 900 miles or so apart. Indeed, the connection is the "Thoroughbred." My life long interest in seeing the "undervalued" do well moved me to write about some bargain yearlings that went on to fame. This is my third book, the second to be published. I am excited about this writing. It is a great feeling to write about a subject or subjects, that creates in me the desire to stretch my curiosity well beyond what would be considered normal.

I shared with you the background for this book. I am very fortunate to have an interest in writing. My book on Cape Ann drew me very close to the inhabitants, and for that I am grateful. I feel strongly that this book will draw me much closer to the people of Saratoga and Lexington. It's a good feeling.

I have titled this book "More of Everything Else." As with my second book, it then becomes attached to "Everything Else," the final division of time in my initial writing, a chronicle titled "Reflections," "Chronology," to the "Present." I hope you enjoy the book.

Part I

For Me A Journey

More of Everything Else

1. 1960 — And Then Some

I remember that warm afternoon in June of 1960. It was two weeks before my scheduled graduation from Albany Business College in Albany, New York. I drove to Saratoga Springs this particular day, having been referred by the job placement section at school to apply for a position in Saratoga.

The job was in public relations as Assistant to Howard de Freitas, Director of Public Relations for Saratoga Harness Racing Association Inc. There were two other students from my class applying for the position. I indicated on my application that I had done some writing in high school and later as a member of the United States Air Force.

Apparently, this impressed de Freitas and Fred Betts, Assistant to Frank Wiswall, President of Saratoga Harness. I was notified by phone two days later that I had the job. I graduated from Albany Business College on June 25th and started work the following Monday.

It was a busy time for me, moving out of my Albany apartment and relocating 30 miles north. I rented a room at the "Lewiston Motor Court," on Route 9, a few miles north of the city. I took a room in the house, a very large structure. Orville and Edna Gehr, the owners, who were originally from Maryland were very nice to me.

In preparation for my move to Saratoga from Albany — I wrote the following poem,

FAREWELL TO PLACE

Two years I've been, now I leave
As in the past, and perhaps not the last
Like the wind, its never-ending weave
I will go out into a new world
Knowing not what shadows to be cast
This my farewell to place
Perhaps I've found my star at last
I leave in sorrow but not regret
For its greener fields I've found
Bad times gone, good time to never forget
To start a new life, what can I expect
It must be wonderful when God settles one
Perhaps my time has come, I shall welcome
But now, it's farewell to place.

-A poem I wrote on June 19, 1960

I will always remember my early days in Saratoga, eating meals at the "Triangle" diner, the "G & G" restaurant on Broadway and the horsemen's place, located in the barn area at Saratoga Harness. I enjoyed my work, spending my days working in the office and at night, in the press box, "way -a — top — the — grandstand." At night I operated the teletype, sending the feature race highlights and race results to area newspapers. The cities of Albany, Troy, Schenectady, Glens Falls in New York and Bennington, Vermont were among the areas receiving my communication. I always enjoyed observing George Miller, the track announcer call the races.

In the fall of 1960, I began to circulate in the community. In time I joined the "Saratoga Chorus," the local chapter of SPEBSQSA, the society for barbershop quartet singing in America. I had done a great deal of singing in high school, and truly enjoyed it. I also became a patron of the "Colonial Tavern" located at 340 Broadway. My favorite listener in those days was Pat Cruise, the bartender. As I look back on my earlier days in Saratoga, I can honestly admit that I felt a strong attachment for this historic community.

I later met and married Marjorie Johnson, a local Saratoga girl who lived at 77 White Street on the east side of town. At the time of our marriage, I was back living in Utica, having accepted a position with a local financial institution. Our first daughter Ann was born on December 25, 1965. On November 12, 1970 our second daughter Julie Ann arrived.

As mentioned, despite having only lived in Saratoga for a short time, I felt strongly attached, and being married to a native made it easy for me to learn a great deal about the city's history. We were very fortunate to spend our August vacations each year at the spa. My late father-in-law, Gerald M. Johnson owned together with his brother Moylan the "Hygrade Market," on Caroline Street.

I always enjoyed listening to Margie's dad talk about old Saratoga; he had many stories to tell. For years we stayed at 77 White Street, during our visits. I will never forget the times when Margie's dad allowed us to rent rooms in the 13 room house. Margie used to deal with "Bugs" over at the "Reading Room," on Union Avenue. When we were renting rooms, the four of us would sleep on the sofa bed in the second living room. My daughters used to call it the "funny bed."

The 1960's were exciting years for Saratoga. In 1961, Saratoga Performing Arts Center was first proposed. The reason behind this proposal was a concern that historic Saratoga would be inundated with sport lovers and horseplayers. There was a need for an element of culture at the "Spa." The patrons of the arts responded with enthusiasm and donations. The state of New York supplied $960,000 of the original estimate of $2.4 million.

In the summer of 1963 Saratoga remembered the opening of Saratoga Racecourse with a centennial celebration. My old barbershop friends, the Saratoga Chorus, participated in the opening ceremonies.

On June 30, 1964, a crowd of 1,000 Saratogians watched as Governor Rockefeller climbed on the seat of a tractor and plowed up a plot of turf to break ground for the "Performing Arts Center." Eugene Ormondy, Conductor of the Philadelphia Orchestra and Lincoln Kirstein, of the New York City Ballet, two future tenants were on hand. The center would be designed as an amphitheater accommodating 5,100 people with space for 7,000 more on the surrounding sloping grounds. The ballet would perform in July and the orchestra during the month of August.

A few months into the project, it was obvious that the actual cost would be greater than the initial estimate. In the summer of 1965, members of the horse society rode to the rescue. Names like: Alfred C. Vanderbilt, John Hay Whitney (N.Y. Tribune), Mrs. Charles Payson (N.Y. Mets), Mrs. Gene Markey (Calumet Farms), Mrs. Elizabeth Graham (Elizabeth Arden Cosmetics).

In time, the elite put together a benefit ball, resulting in a sizeable contribution. Soon the balance needed to satisfy the $4 million cost was raised. In the summer of 1966 the Saratoga Performing Arts Center (SPAC) opened.

In the late 1960's I began to faithfully attend the annual August yearling sales. The sales were held the second week of racing, conducted by the Fasig - Tipton Company, a company formed in 1898 by William B. Fasig and Ed A. Tipton. The company has been part of Saratoga's August scene since 1920. I really began to take a greater interest in the sales during the 1970's and the early part of the following decade. I would look forward to those four evenings in August. This period in time was a period when the prices just kept going up and up and up. There seemed to be no limit on the amount people would pay for an untried yearling.

The August 4, 1975 edition of the "Daily Racing Form" printed a message from Governor Hugh L. Carey. In his letter, the Governor stated; "The Saratoga sales contribute to the greatness of Saratoga racing. This is a proud sale where the finest horses are to be seen. The sales are important to Thoroughbred racing, one of New York's great industries."

Governor Carey was a strong supporter of the breeding side of the horse business, and was very active in the revitalization of the Thoroughbred Breeding Industry in New York State. He felt that New York, with the finest hay and natural grains to be found anywhere in the country provided a "natural environment" for raising fine horses.

The 1970's proved to be exciting years for the Saratoga yearling sales. On Thursday evening, August 12, 1971 a Buckpasser colt, hip number 136 sold for a record price of $235,000. And from that point in time, going forward to the mid 1980's, the breeding side of the Thoroughbred industry would enjoy a period of "boom" times.

I was in attendance the night of August 7, 1973 when Leroy Jolley purchased hip number 53, for $20,000 a bargain price for this bay colt, the grandson of Bold Ruler and Tom Fool. This colt, as I mentioned in the preface was later named Foolish Pleasure and accomplished great things. Six years later on August 9, 1979 a bay colt by Foolish Pleasure sold for $200,000 — 10 times the amount paid for the sire. That same night, hip number 159, a Sir Ivor colt sold for $650,000 and number 173, a Raise A Native filly went for $350,000.

A year earlier, August 10, 1978, I recall the sale of hip number 137, a Nijinsky colt for $800,000. The total sale in 1978 amounted to $17 million, an increase from $10 million in 1976 and $12.1 million in 1977. By 1979 the figure grew to $20 million for an average price of $98,000. I was at the sales the evening of August 7, 1980 when a bay filly by The Minstrel brought $900,000, the top price for the four day sale. The next entry into the Humphrey S. Finney Pavilion, hip number 169, a Damascus filly sold for $165,000. The 1980 sale came in at $25.9 million with an average price of $111,159.

In 1982, four tense evenings of selling saw a total of $36.1 million being disbursed for 204 colts and fillies. Sheik Mohammed bin Rashid al Maktun, an Arab established a record price for a filly by paying $2.1 million for a daughter of The Minstrel.

Life is full of change, and the horse industry is no exception to this rule. In the mid 80's the yearling sales peaked. The year 1986 brought tax law changes, that resulted in horses no longer being used as tax shelters. This brought an end to the $500,000 stud fees, throwing the industry into a tailspin. I will treasure the memories of those nights, standing on the outside of the Humphrey S. Finney Pavilion, observing the activity inside or viewing the auction on the outside monitors. In addition to my recollection of the many yearlings sold over the years, there are other memories with respect to the Fasig - Tipton sales. I was there on August 8, 1974, when at 9:00 P.M. the gavel was silenced as Richard M. Nixon resigned the office of President of the United States. The President read the following statement. "Therefore, I shall resign the presidency, effective at noon tomorow. Vice President Ford will be sworn in as President at that hour in this office."

I used to enjoy a drink or two at the bar of the Spuyten Duyvil, a Saratoga nightspot located next to the Humphrey S. Finney sales pavilion. I recall being in there one evening, when by chance the owner had asked a paying guest to play the baby grand piano, located just off the bar area. It was a great experience, the guest turned out to be Andre Previn. One night Margie and I were at the sales, to my surprise, standing next to us was Harry James, the great trumpet player. As a lot of people might know, Harry James was also an owner of Thoroughbreds.

I referred earlier to my late father - in -law, Gerald M. Johnson, part owner of the Hygrade Market located just off Broadway at the corner of Caroline Street and Maple Avenue. Jerry Johnson, as everyone, including his grandchildren called him used to love to talk about Saratoga's past. He knew a lot about the history of Saratoga; in fact at one time was asked by Saratoga native Frank Sullivan, the late humorist with the "New Yorker Magazine" to collaborate a writing on "events and happenings" in Saratoga over the years.

The Hygrade Market at the time of its closing in 1964 was the oldest butcher shop in the city. It had operated in the "valley" section of town for 40 years. The market came into being in 1924 when J. Moylan Johnson, the older brother opened a butcher shop. My father-in-law joined him-three years later. Prior to the meat market, their father, Matthew had operated a tavern in the building. My research disclosed that the saloon had opened in the early 1900s and that a man named Daniel A'Hearn ran a fish market on the north section of the building. I recall Margie's dad telling a story about a murder that occurred in the early 1900s up over the fish market. According to what I remember, a man named "Smith" was killed by a man named "Hogabone" in a dispute over a card game.

I am not sure how old the Hygrade Market building was, but remember Jerry saying it was built prior to 1850. The store flourished in the 1930s, with eight full time butchers. I used to love to hear him recall the experiences of catering to the gambling casinos, nightclubs and the many millionaires that took up residence every August. The corner of Caroline Street and Maple Avenue is today a parking lot.

The Johnson brothers had seven children. My wife, Margie was one of four girls. Moylan Johnson had a son, Matt, and two daughters. People used to kid about Matt Johnson, saying he was the son that Margie's father never had. Matt used to spend a lot of time at the Hygrade, when he wasn't hustling race track programs on Broadway or parking cars on his father's side lawn, or Uncle Jerry's parking lot. Margie's dad owned a lot, just opposite the Wright Street entrance to the big track. Margie and her three sisters all had a shot at parking cars during the August meet. At one time, Matt had an interest in a career at the Hygrade, but in the late 1950s and early 1960s, the super market chain stores were slowly replacing the small markets. The brothers encouraged Matt to consider something else, and he did. For a period of five years he worked under Eddy Corey, the "Steward" for Harry M. Stevens Company, the firm that handled the culinary activities at many race tracks, and other sports arenas. During that period of time, Matt worked at "Tropical Park," "Gulfstream," "Hialeagh," and "Saratoga." He later entered a long career as a sales representative for a large meat packer.

As a youth, Matt recalls many prominent Saratoga residents that patronized the Hygrade. Dr. and Mrs. Magovern, "Doc" Sullivan, the Veterinarian and Al Smith (the numbers man), to name a few. Al Smith worked for Al Pepper, who ran the gambling room at Newman's Lake House out on Saratoga Lake. Newman's was one of the many establishments shut down as a result of the famed Kefauver Investigation into organized crime and corruption in the 1950s. Matt remembers some of the other store fronts that made up the part of Caroline Street that began at Maple Avenue. A shoe repair shop, "S. Ventre," was closest to the market. The next store was "Brophy's," with a large "Coca Cola" sign in front. Matt laughed when he told me that John Brophy used to "make book" at the rear of the store.

In the heat of summer, during the racing season the butcher shop was staffed with 11 or 12 meat cutters. I can only go back to 1961 with personal memories of the Hygrade, and from that point to the closing in 1964.

I do recall that after the store closed in 1964, Margie's dad tended bar at Sperry's, a bar located opposite the Hygrade on Caroline Street. I used to go with him on occasion to Sperry's for a good sandwich and a few beers. We used to visit with "Geyser Dick," the regular bartender. Sperry's is still a part of Caroline Street, but it is now a very popular restaurant. It doesn't resemble the Sperry's I once knew. Margie's dad always enjoyed talking about the Hygrade and 40 years of catering to the public. He would often say, "people knew how to buy meat then, today they strap you to a cart and basket, and you deal with packaged meat."

An article that appeared May 26, 1993 in the Saratogian offered a clear picture of Caroline Street as it was in 1952. Martha Stonequist, city historian writes that the street, starting at Broadway was a shoppers paradise.

There was Holland's Printing and Gifts, Lewis Market and the New York Bargain Store. Then, Grant's Lunch, Jim's Shoe Shine and Hat Hospital (interesting). As you continue walking the north side of Caroline there was Rose Dress Shop, Mc Laughlin's Liquor Store and at the corner of Maple Avenue, opposite the "Hygrade" was DeFrehn, a jeweler. On the south side of Caroline were many other business establishments, a beauty shop, tailor shop and a barber shop.

The places I remember on Caroline Street when I first arrived in 1960 were The Inn, owned by Bud Brophy and the Turf bar. My favorite

place today, Gaffney's is located near where the Turf bar was located years ago. The Inn is long gone too.

I found the article very interesting, and after reading it could better relate to Margie's dad always saying that Caroline Street was the center of activity.

I believe growing up in Saratoga would have been a fun experience. As a young boy in Utica, New York I experienced baseball, golf, paper route, all that kind of activity, but having a "big league" race track in your hometown offers a different kind of excitement.

I had lunch with Fred Lewis on October 5, 1996 at Gaffney's on Caroline Street. I needed to get a feel for what it was like to grow up around the "spa." I met Fred in August of 1996, while he was working with Bob Duncan, official starter for the New York Racing Association. He was referred to me by a mutual friend, "Pepper Beloin," a jockey for Brandywine Stables back in the 1950's.

I asked Fred to share with me some of his experiences, going back to the time he left the family farm at age 14. His early experiences included shining shoes on Saratoga's historic "Broadway." The going rate was 20 cents, often enhanced by a 5 cents tip. It could get better, like the time Keith Stewart the jockey gave him a dollar for a boot shine. Ames O'Brien the "numbers" man used to throw him a five dollar bill. Wow!

At age 15, the sound of hoofbeats danced in Fred's head and he received permission from his mother to apply for work as a jockey. His first experience was with Brandywine Stables for a three year period. It was a difficult time, dealing with constant weight adjustment, thus he abandoned this role. Fred later worked for the Walter M. Jeffords stable as an exercise boy, followed by a few years in the United States Army.

In 1962 the race track environment once again attracted his interest. He began a career spanning more than three decades with the NYRA as an assistant starter and schooling horses. For many years, Fred worked under George Cassidy, the official starter at "Aqueduct,"

"Belmont," and "Saratoga." Though now retired, Fred continues to be part of the Saratoga scene —— moving back to the area and working the August meet.

I know from my own personal experiences that a long time in any career offers an opportunity to witness change. I asked Fred about that. This was something I asked the many people I interviewed for my book on Cape Ann.

In Fred's case, he always enjoyed getting to know the many owners when they would mingle in the backstretch years ago. With time, and the passing of generations, there seems to be less opportunity for that, according to Fred. In addition, he sees a difference in attitude on the part of the people handling the horses. In the old days, "how the horse looked" was very important. I shared with him that this is the way life is today; the pride in what we do is not always there. At least as I see it. Too bad!

Fred shared with me that he enjoyed his many years as part of the NYRA team. He continued by recalling some names from years past, famous people he rubbed elbows with. As a fan of the National Football League, one particular story is easy for him to remember. One morning he arrived for work at Belmont and spotted two former NFL greats engaged in casual conversation with Lucien Laurin, trainer of Secretariat regarding schooling of their horses. Pat Fischer, all pro cornerback with the Cardinals and Redskins and Billy Kilmer who played with San Francisco, New Orleans and Washington were, in Fred's mind totally relaxed. It kind of took Fred by surprise, as in his mind, he could see them in the "heat of battle" on the gridiron.

For sure, being part of the "race track" scene for a long time provides a natural for being around celebrities. To name a few, Fred shared with me the names of Mickey Rooney, Candace Bergen, Cab Calloway, Jack Klugman and Reba McEntire of country music fame.

It was obvious to me that Fred and I both shared a warm regard for the city of Saratoga Springs. I continued our conversation by mentioning the fact I used to travel to New York City a great deal when I was working. I shared with him that on more than one occasion I would be engaged in dialogue, perhaps with a bartender at my favorite steak house "Gallagher's" on West 52nd, regarding Saratoga. It never failed, Leo or Tom, my favorite bartenders had their own personal "Saratoga" experiences to talk about.

One thing is for sure — there are not too many people out there that have not experienced "Saratoga" in August.

Frank Sullivan, the late humorist lived practically all his life at 135 Lincoln Avenue, just around the corner from Margie's house at 77 White Street. Sullivan was born in 1892, attended local schools and worked as a cub reporter for the Saratogian, prior to entering Cornell University. After graduating from Cornell, he served in the army until 1919 when he travelled to New York City.

Frank Sullivan worked the next twelve years for three New York papers, "The Herald," "The Evening Sun," and "The World." From its beginning in 1925, he was a contributor to "The New Yorker" magazine.

I recall Margie's dad talking about Frank Sullivan often, sort of reminiscing about past trips to New York City with Margie's mom and Dr. and Mrs. Magovern. One of their favorite places was "Toots Shors," where they would enjoy the friendship of Frank Sullivan and others, including Pat O'Brien, the movie actor.

Margie's dad was a great story teller, and was blessed with a great memory for past events. He had a lot of love for the city of Saratoga, as did Frank Sullivan. The April 29, 1951 issue of the New York Times Magazine section printed an article by Sullivan that was quite interesting. The article, titled "A Saratogian Defends Saratoga," offered the reader a lot of reasons to believe Saratoga was a sinless city until the August visitors arrived.

It was obvious at the time that Sullivan's article was aimed at Senator Kefauver's Committee on organized crime that shut down the Saratoga casinos. In 1951 the population of Saratoga was 15,000.

Sullivan's article reflects on the fact that Saratoga was perhaps different than any other city of that size. He stated, "it is more tolerant." And, he was right, because even today for a period of six to eight weeks each year Saratoga is a source of entertainment for a variety of Americans, numbering in the thousands.

It was a good article, and it reminded me of how Margie's dad used to tell how he would restrict the activities of his four daughters during the month of August; in other words, keep them close to the front porch.

I have to say at this point that Saratoga has played a major role in my life, and that it will always be very important to me. I am not a gambler, although I will wander to the pari-mutuel window on occasion. I love to view the Thoroughbreds from the first turn at Saratoga, just leaning on the fence. I also enjoy seeing them work out in the morning while having breakfast. My biggest thrill is seeing the many yearlings that are brought to Saratoga every August for the purpose of being auctioned off.

I believe, as evidenced by this book that Saratoga will always be a part of me. A great place!

More of Everything Else

2. Saratoga

I knew little about the city of Saratoga Springs prior to my moving there in 1960. I was aware that it was an area deep in history, popular for its mineral springs, resort hotels and a beautiful race track.

For sure there is much more to it than that. In the early days, Saratoga was spelled many different ways: "Cheratoga," "Sarachtioge," "Saragtoga," "Sarachtoga' "Saractoga," "Saroghtoga," "Saratoge," Saraktoga," "Sarasrogue," "Sarasteau," "Schorachtoge," "Saraston," "Saratogo," "SearchTague," "Sarrantau," "Seraghtoga," "Soraghtoga. Certain old maps also refer to it as So-roeto-gos-land. Can you believe that?

It was obvious from my research that certain historians liked one or two versions of the spelling, with some degree of justification for their choice. In any event, the name has, from colonial times, referred to a region extending forty three miles north and south and some twenty-eight miles east and west which on February 17, 1791 was set off from Albany County as Saratoga County.

By natural process it also applied specifically to the sparkling lake eight miles west of the settlement on the Hudson and to the celebrated watering place which grew up around the saline springs four miles farther away.

Saratoga County is in the foothills of the Adirondacks. Two deep, narrow valleys form an angle within which the county lies. One of these valleys stretches four hundred miles between the islands of

Montreal and Manhattan. The other leads west from the mouth of the Mohawk River to the basin of the Great Lakes.

Until the seventeenth century the Iroquois (Six Nations) a confederation of North American Indian Tribes were in power. Their numerous enemies, mainly Algonquins in the valley of the St. Lawrence and Abenaquis and Montaqnais from beyond the Saquenay were no real match for them. The Iroquois spread a path of influence combined with bloodshed and destruction along the trails they travelled, including Saratoga County.

In 1609 Samuel de Champlain, founder of Quebec and the first governor of Canada explored south to Crown Point. Henry Hudson, the English navigator, seeking the East Indies for his employer came up his namesake river to Waterford, which is situated at the southern tip of Saratoga County.

For a 30 year period the Indians forbid white men to travel the country between Waterford and Crown Point. This did not, however stop the Dutch who in 1624 established a trading post at Fort Orange (now Albany). There were those who tried to break down the barriers. The first to do so was Isaac Jogues, the Jesuit missionary.. Father Jogues was captured by the Iroquois in 1642 at the age of 35. He was tortured and made a slave.

The French and Indian Wars, the name applied to four wars between the French and English in America had an impact on the Saratoga region. In 1666 the Marquis de Tracey passed within four or five miles of what is now Saratoga Springs, while leading thirteen hundred French and Indians to the sack of the Mohawk Castles near Schoharie Creek and Tribes Hill. In1689 fifteen hundred Iroquois crossed Saratoga Lake on their way to Montreal.

In 1690, a group of French soldiers, with Canadian Indians at their side stopped at the house of Bartle Vroman long enough to gather three scalps. Vroman's house was believed to be the first house erected in Saratoga County. Local historians strongly felt the first blow struck west of the Atlantic in King Williams War was landed at old Saratoga, (now Schuylerville).

King William's War was the first of the four war series, known as the French and Indian War. It began in 1689, when William and Mary ascended the throne of England.

Queen Anne's War, the second in the series began in 1702 when the war of the Spanish Succession commenced in Europe. James Moore of South Carolina, with a force of Whites and Indians destroyed several Spanish settlements in Florida. This war brought English military forces into the region of Saratoga. They built a stockade fort at old Saratoga (now Schuylerville), and from there they made a road along the east side of the river, connecting with the Great Carrying Place, now known as Fort Edward.

Philip Pieterson Schuyler arrived from Amsterdam in 1650. The Schuyler family, mainly composed of solid, practical, rather unimaginative folk was for a long time the most important family in Saratoga County. Together with Robert Livingston, Albany Town Clerk, the Schuylers obtained land grants from the Indians as early as 1683. They established the first organized settlement soon after the turn of the eighteenth century. By 1745 the mills that Captain John Philip Schuyler had erected at the outlet of Saratoga Lake were doing a tidy business.

Along about that time, the third war in the series of four was in progress. King George's War began in 1744 when the war of the Austrian Succession commenced in Europe. This war impacted the Saratoga region as well. On November 16, 1745 a strong French raiding party originally headed for the Connecticut Valley passed through and attacked the Saratoga region doing major damage to the stockade.

In 1746 a new fort was erected but was attacked in June of 1747, and ordered to be dismantled. Soon after, Albany became the extreme northern outpost of the English.

Sir William Johnson arrived in this country in 1738 at the age of 23. Some eight years later he became Commissary of New York for Indian Affairs. The Iroquois held him in high regard, for his efforts to unite two peoples together. By the year 1763, the year that peace finally

33

came, the men and women of the Saratoga region began a long period of time rebuilding their properties. At the same time they would prepare for a new war which would demonstrate the importance of the region.

The Indians had earned a reputation for being gossipy and eager to share information. If there is an exception to this, it perhaps would involve the marvelous curative properties of the spring which spouted out of a rock near Saratoga. It is amazing that for two centuries, no white man was known to have seen the spring.

In 1767, suffering from the gout and the effects of an earlier bullet wound, Sir William Johnson was being assisted by Thayendanega, the Mohawk chief, with whom he was closely associated. The Mohawks brought him down the Mohawk River to Schenectady by boat, and then carried him on a litter to the spring. He stayed four days, sleeping in a bark hut and taking baths. It is believed he was the first white man to use the spring. In addition it is written that it offered relief to his suffering.

That particular spring, referred to as High Rock Spring is located in downtown Saratoga Springs. An area of the Saratoga region, embracing Saratoga Springs and Saratoga Lake is an area referred to as Kay-ad-ros-se-ra. It means the land of the beautiful lake of the winding river. In 1764 several families settled where Lake Saratoga joins Kayaderosseras Creek. There was concern on the part of the Indians, because this was a popular hunting ground for them.

In 1768, after much negotiating, the Iroquois Confederacy on behalf of the Mohawks retained much of the hunting ground. A share of the land passed to Rip Van Dam and subsequently became the village of Saratoga Springs. In 1763 Michael and Nicholas Mc Donald, brothers from the north of Ireland had settled in an area called Ballston, just south of the springs at Saratoga.

The first hostilities between the continentals and the British regulars broke out on April 19, 1775 at Lexington, Massachusetts. On

May 10, 1775 the Second Continental Congress petitioned the King and British people to make amends, but prepared for war. George Washington was selected as the Commander in Chief of the Continental Army. The Declaration of Independence was adopted by a unanimous vote on July 4, 1776, naming the new nation, United States of America. Most of the seaport cities were captured by the British, but the Americans held the interior and recaptured some of the cities.

The first decisive battle and the one which is considered the turning point of the Revolutionary War occurred at old Saratoga (now Schuylerville).

The battle comprised two engagements in which the British fought under General John Burgoyne and the Americans under General Horatio Gates. Trying to occupy the Hudson Valley and to cut off the New England colonists from the rest of their Countrymen, the British advanced to an area near Stillwater.

The first attack was on September 19,1777. There were 300 American casualties and 600 British. Burgoyne attacked again on October 7, 1777. That day, the British, after encountering around 700 casualties withdrew to Saratoga. Besieged in Saratoga, Burgoyne signed the Convention of Saratoga on October 17, 1777, pledging that his forces would not serve against the Americans again. The British troops were marched to Boston and returned to England.

The Battle of Saratoga convinced the French to give aid to the Americans. On February 6, 1778 a treaty alliance between France and the United States was signed. Six thousand troops were sent to aid Washington. Eventually, George Washington, heading up an American French army defeated a British army under the direction of Lord Cornwallis at Yorktown, Virginia. This virtually ended the war.

In 1782 the British abandoned the southern ports and held only New York. The Treaty of Peace was signed at Versailles in 1783. There were many volunteers from Massachusetts and Connecticut and elsewhere who had rallied to the cause at Saratoga. Upon returning to their houses, many were convinced that they should uproot and settle back in the Saratoga area. They worked hard at convincing others to travel to Saratoga for a glimpse of this almost fabled land.

Amos Stafford, who at the age of nineteen had fought British and Indians, arrived in 1783. He settled on Fish Creek, the outlet to Saratoga Lake. Samuel Waterbury arrived some years later with his brother William from Stamford, Connecticut. There were others: John Arnold, his wife Martha and son John came from Rhode Island.

Gideon Putnam, son of Stephen and Mary Gibbs Putnam was born in Sutton, Massachusetts in the year 1763. As a young man Gideon wandered from Massachusetts to Middlebury, Vermont and then to Rutland, Vermont. Restless, he moved again, this time to Five Nations, or Bemis Flats in the Saratoga Region. He soon became restless once again, and with his young bride, Doanda relocated to High Rock. It was here that he knew he belonged — recognizing the value of the mineral springs and the timber.

In time, new springs were discovered; Congress, Flat Rock, Red to name a few. And there was increasing evidence that there were more. By now many considered Gideon Putnam a prophet. As the nineteenth century began to unfold, Gideon began to expand on his dream. In 1802 he arranged for the felling and hewing of tall pines which grew thick upon an acre of land that he had purchased from the Surrogate of Saratoga County. He erected a frame building seventy feet long. The structure became three stories high and twenty four feet deep. It contained a large dining room, two parlors, and a spacious kitchen. The second and third stories were designed for lodging. A sign was posted "Putnam's Tavern and Boarding House."

There were those that believed Gideon had made an error in judgement as to the potential for attracting visitors to the area he had grown to love. Gideon, the prophet paid no heed, and he continued to live his dream. In 1803 improvements and additions became necessary at the great house. By this time six springs were known to exist within a half mile of High Rock. Gideon Putnam was now convinced he had made the right decision in building his great house.

It would not be long before increased activity would lead to new developments in the region. With signs of additional springs, digging eight to ten feet often resulted in mineral water rising from among the stones and gravel.

Gideon Putnam died on December 1, 1812 from lung complications resulting from an accident the year before. He was survived by his wife Doanda and five sons and four daughters. These heirs took over the great house and because of their love for the community, it came to be known as Union Hall. In 1864, it was renamed Grand Union. The successors to Gideon's role as helmsman came from the Commonwealth of Massachusetts and Connecticut. It was not long before "society" held considerable presence within Saratoga Springs. This did not, however eliminate the presence of other factions, described as rum purveyors and visiting dupes.

Saratoga soon earned a reputation for its "spas," and was called the "Queen of Spas." The "upper village" consisted of buildings clustered near High Rock. Farther south and composed mainly of several hotels near Congress Spring, the section was called the "lower village."

Saratoga continued to be recognized for its springs and other attractions for the visitor. Union Hall had grown 120 feet long, with two wings extending west sixty feet. Congress Hall was now 200 feet long and three stories high. In 1824 Elias Benedict built the United States Hotel, accommodating up to 150 guests. For some forty pre Civil War years politicians of all degrees, both those who practiced in Albany and those seeking surcease from their labors in Washington or other state capitols found Saratoga Springs a pleasant place to converse. This was also a time in history when gambling in America experienced a period of great growth. During these flush times poker, craps, faro, monte and a variety of other games of chance were extremely popular.

Saratoga was now an attraction for the very wealthy, and would soon lead to breaking the barrier that limited large scale gambling to hotel rooms. Gambling came out in the open and in 1842 Ben Scribner opened the first house exclusively for that purpose. Five years later, Patton and Cole, owners of a bowling alley and shooting gallery near Washington Spring announced the city of Saratoga would have a race-course. This was to be a half-mile trotting track and would be located across Union Avenue from the present track.

And so Saratoga continued to flourish with some degree of fluctuation — as the wealthy resisted the public gaming activities, preferring to gamble in the privacy of their hotel rooms. Then came the Civil War in 1860. The first shot of the war was fired by the south against Fort Sumter on April 12, 1861. The war between the north and south continued for four hard years, with the end occurring on April 9, 1865 when General Robert E. Lee the Confederate leader surrendered to General Ulysses Simpson Grant, the Union leader at Appomattox County Virginia. Grant would later become the 18th. President of the United States. His "Memoirs" were written at his cottage at Mount McGregor, just north of Saratoga Springs.

The Civil War brought John Morrissey to Saratoga Springs, but even without a war he probably would have come. Morrissey, as a youth in Troy, just south of the "spa" knew this was the place to which the nice people fled in summer time. He had always wanted to be "nice people," so in 1861 he came to Saratoga Springs.

John Morrissey was born of Irish peasantry and at the age of three was brought to the land of opportunity. His background was varied, and included serving as a deck hand on a river boat, gang fighter, bouncer in a saloon-brothel—then advancing to heavyweight champion of America. The title came under the London Prize Ring Rules.

Morrissey, by the age of 35 had experienced success in the political arena, and at that tender age was elected to Congress. Along the way John Morrissey had experienced success as a gaming-house proprietor. He had established locations in New York City. The Gem Saloon on Broadway and the Bella Union on Leonard Street were two that brought him financial gain. In 1854 he became a leader of the Tammany Hall faction, serving as a key backer to Fernando Wood, a millionaire ship owner and candidate for Mayor.

Morrissey remained in New York enjoying a life of "elegance" and accumulating a great deal of wealth and power. In 1861, after the start of the Civil War he set out to advance his personal ambition. He travelled to Saratoga with roulette wheels, faro layouts, suave dealers and strong armed attendants. They settled down on Matilda Street (now Woodlawn Ave), near Broadway and the best hotels.

Morrissey enjoyed immediate success with his latest venture. Ben Scribner's modest resort had no chance in competition with the well appointed establishment where the limit of play customarily was dictated by the desires of the patrons. In fact, soon after, Scribner went to work for Morrissey.

The war continued, as did the profits for Morrissey. The "nice" people were very important to him — and finding ways to entertain them, in turn made Morrissey an important part of their lives.

On August 3, 1863 Saratoga Springs first running horse track opened. This was Morrissey's attempt to ease the unrest of his patrons. It was not the only track operating during these parlous times. Lexington, Kentucky, indeed, had continued to race with the exception of one meeting. The track in 1862 had been converted to a resting site for a group of Confederate soldiers.

It was obvious to Morrissey that he needed assistance for this new venture. William R. Travers, member of twenty-seven clubs, excellent judge of wines and foods, wealthy broker and New York society's favorite wit, became President of the Racing Association. John R. Hunter and Leonard W. Jerome, grandfather of the renowed British statesman, Winston Churchill, came on board as additional assistance.

The inaugural four-day meeting at the new track began August 2, 1864, while the Union armies were moving in on Petersburg and Atlanta. The Travers Stakes, named in honor of the association president was run for the first time at this meeting. The first Travers was won by Kentucky under the colors of William R. Travers.

The track was later enlarged and placed at a different angle. Horse Haven, the 1863 track remains, and is used for early morning workouts.

John Morrissey was an interesting person, many times provoking citizen comments of praise and shame in the same breath. One such comment, "the Honorable John is liked in Saratoga because he divides the profits of his sinning with the good people of the village with generous hand."

In 1867 work began on the Club House which would be situated on terraced lawns with elm shaded approaches in the Congress Spring area. The large public gaming room was on the first floor and provided ample facilities for faro and roulette, the most popular banking games of that period.

Upstairs there were private rooms where the heavy hitters could indulge themselves without being annoyed by the presence of lesser suckers. Such nationally eminent Republicans as Simon Cameron, boss of Pennsylvania, Zach Chandler of Michigan and General Robert Schenk of Ohio were three frequent challengers of Morrissey at the poker table.

From the beginning, Morrissey barred women from the gaming rooms. It was reported that the cost to Morrissey for building the Club House including landscaping the grounds was $190,000. There was a period of time when strong resistance to the gambling efforts was evidenced from time to time. The "North American Review" in 1868 printed, "the high whirl of Newport and Saratoga" serves as a ready Lethe for all moral obligations."

The resistance took shape in the form of certain fires designed to wipe out the town. The first of these holocausts occurred on July 4, 1864. A powder cracker was tossed into a water cure establishment, touching off lace curtains. In 1883 a permanent paid fire department was organized, offering an increased comfort level for residents with respect to fear of fire.

John Morrissey enjoyed a great deal of good living, to the point his weight had increased to 226 pounds. In time he returned to the political arena by being elected to the New York State Senate. In April of 1878, Morrissey died as a result of a stroke of paralysis aggravated by other ailments. The New York legislature adjourned upon hearing the news. Flags flew at half staff. It is said that at least twice in his life he was a millionaire. When his estate was settled, it amounted to less than $75,000.

There were others that impacted Saratoga's gambling scene in a big way. Richard Albert Canfield was born in New Bedford, Massachusetts on June 17, 1855, one of six children. As a young man Canfield drew attention as a skilled gambler. He performed as a free lance gambler in Boston, Pawtucket and Providence.

In 1877 Richard Canfield took a position as night clerk at the prosperous Union Square Hotel in New York City. Andrew J. Dam, a cousin of his mother from New Bedford was the proprietor of the hotel. While working at the Union Square he met and was accepted by many celebrities. Maurice Barrymore, Steele Mac Kaye, Albert J. Simmons, the Boston Railroad man and Loren N. Downs of New England Telephone Company were a few of his gambling friends. All four had earned a reputation as big time gamblers.

For the next few years Canfield was involved in several gambling ventures, including one that caused him to reduce his activities to a crawl. In 1885 Canfield, along with his partner Thomas Sprague and an employee of the Sprague-Canfield Establishment in Providence were sentenced to a six month jail term for promoting illegal gambling.

By 1892 Canfield was one of the best regarded gamblers in New York City and was reported to be worth around a million dollars. By this time he had frequented Saratoga Springs many times and had grown to love it. Albert Spencer, one of the principals in the Club House after John Morrissey's death, had taken a real fancy toward Canfield. By 1893 the Club House was showing signs of financial difficulty and Canfield was aware of it. Spencer and Canfield reached an agreement, and Canfield bought a part of the operation for the 1893 season. Despite competition from the Chicago Worlds Fair and poor economic conditions nationwide, the Club House turned a fair profit that year.

In 1894 the start of the most dazzling decade in Saratoga's gambling history began. Canfield introduced some changes at the Club House. He hired the noted French chef, Jean Columbin and paid him $5,000 for the two month season. At the end of a season, Columbin would use an expense account provided by Canfield and travel to Europe for the purpose of picking up food ideas for use in Saratoga.

The people who visited Saratoga during the last half of the nineteenth century and the twentieth century were to include some of the most famous in the land. General Daniel E. Sickles, the powerful Republican member of Congress was a familiar figure. John Graham and Abe Hummell, famous criminal lawyers used to patronize Saratoga's hot spots. Frank James, brother of outlaw Jesse James attended the races in Saratoga. Elihu Root, a graduate of Hamilton College who served as Secretary of War and later Secretary of State in 1905 was a frequent visitor. Root was the recipient of the Nobel Peace Prize in 1912.

In addition, Lillian Russell the operatic soprano used to drive through the streets of Saratoga in a carriage drawn by two prancing black horses. In 1902, Richard Canfield purchased from the Kilmer estate, property adjoining the Club House grounds. He hired Clarence Luce, the eminent New York architect to design a casino that could be built and ready for the 1903 season.

There were people in Saratoga that did not support Canfield's intention to build the casino. This was due to problems he had encountered in New York City with respect to running a gaming operation. As it turned out the casino began to attract visitors even before it officially opened. In June, Canfield took a large party of friends and reporters on a tour. They were very impressed.

The casino was situated next to Congress Spring Park, a tranquil site of curving walks, benches, ponds and the Congress Spring.

Once inside the casino the visitor came upon a variety of treats. One wall of the public gaming room was paneled with mirrors, with statuettes of renowned Frenchmen standing between them on marble pedestals. Glittering chandeliers dropped from the ceiling, and underfoot was a $10,000, 72 x 44 foot rug from Scotland. It was believed to be the largest rug ever woven in one piece.

The restaurant included a vast European style dining room with octagonal stained glass windows in a vaulted ceiling. In 1904 the Saratoga authorities notified the gaming proprietors that they would be enforcing new restrictions. There would be a need for the gambling activities to be conducted in almost total secrecy. In Canfield's mind, he was better off to close the casino. And he did. In time, gambling was only carried on in private hotel rooms. In 1907 Canfield's wealth was estimated at $12 million, a result of gambling and Wall Street investments. In 1911, he sold the casino property for $150,000 to the village of Saratoga Springs, to be retained as a public park.

In 1914, Richard Canfield died as a result of a fractured skull suffered in a fall in a subway. He was 59 years old and worth less than a million dollars at the time of his death. The casinos had all shut down, and the spa was no longer the popular attraction that it was when gambling was widespread. In 1912, Woodrow Wilson was elected to the office of President of the United States. He was elected to a second term in 1916, narrowly winning over Charles E. Hughes. The Democratic slogan, "He kept us out of war," was soon forgotten. On April 6, 1917, America entered the war against Germany. Some eighteen months later the United States had two million troops in Europe.

The war in Europe, described as World War I, ended on November 18, 1918. In time, following the war, the climate for gambling in and about Saratoga was again deemed attractive. The Brook, Arrowhead and Piping Rock were new casinos that had opened in the countryside near Saratoga Lake. All were operated along much the same lines as the Canfield Casino. The exception being that meals were priced lower than Canfield's restaurant. There was big time entertainment, such as Helen Morgan, Sophie Tucker, Ben Bernie and Vincent Lopez.

The 1920's was the dawn of horse racings sunniest era. By that period of time up to 50,000 free spenders annually descended on Saratoga for the season. With that came an increase in the price of anything that carried a price tag. Some of the wealthy began to build their own pleasure palaces while others rented homes for the season. In 1929 the price of a summer cottage ranged from $6,000 to $7,500. The United States Hotel and the Grand Union Hotel were doing a big business too.

Arnold Rothstein, proprietor of the Brook, the casino located just outside town limits had been a regular at Saratoga since 1904. He was the son of wealthy parents, who as a teen ager discovered gambling was profitable enough to make a career of it. And so he did. During the 1920's Rothstein enjoyed a great deal of success. In addition to the Brook and a stable of horses, he was a silent partner in the Chicago Club and several other gambling establishments, He had valuable real estate holdings, prime security investments, large bank account and maintained an expensive apartment on Fifth Avenue in New York City.

In 1919 Rothstein was accused of bribing eight players of the Chicago White Sox to "throw" the World Series. The newspaper labeled it the "Black Sox" scandal and the story was created by the fact that by the time the first series game was to be played, the odds were virtually even. The fact of the matter was that the opponent, the Cincinnati Reds, a highly superior team had previously been the overwhelming favorite by the betting odds. The "Reds" won the series. Rothstein was subpoenaed to answer charges that he was responsible for the deal. His attorney William J. Fallon built a strong case for his innocence and Rothstein claimed he had never in his life been connected to a crooked deal. The jury received this skeptically, but since there was no proof that Rothstein was connected to the conspiracy, he was absolved from any complicity in it.

With that behind him, Rothstein continued to race his horses and operate the Brook. By 1922 a new reform wave rippled over Saratoga, removing officeholders who had become too friendly with gamblers and replaced them with authorities pledged to restore the spa's lost virtue. At the end of the season Rothstein put the Brook on the market and sold it the following year. There were things about Arnold Rothstein that people knew little about. In early 1928, he was shot in the Park Central Hotel in New York City during a card game. It was later disclosed that Rothstein had been very active in underworld activities. This included narcotics, bootleg liquor, and a big money lender and partner to gangsters. At the time of his death, his fortune had mounted to dazzling proportions. His passion for money was never satisfied.

The stock market crash of October 1929 wiped out billions of dollars in paper profits on the stock market and ruined millions of speculators and investors. There were deep faults in America's economic system. Across the country the era of affluence largely sank into a vast Depression. Saratoga refused to be put down.

James C. Young reported in an August 1930 edition of The New York Times that "in a year when everyone has talked of hard times, Saratoga represents a protest." Members of the country's richest club, horse society and others who had survived the financial crash carefully moved forward. In Saratoga, people like William Woodward, John Hay Whitney, Cornelius Vanderbilt Whitney, Pierre Lorillard Sr., John Sanford and Marshall Field partied and enjoyed the racing season.

As the Depression deepened the capers and extravagance displayed at Saratoga were attacked by some observers as tantamount to rubbing salt in the nation's wounds. This resulted in a shifting of attitude on the part of the elite August crowd. Saratoga experienced a mild recession. While society's finest tightened their purse strings, some of the lower status fun seekers took up the slack. It has been recorded that during a time of setback for America, Saratoga was taking in an average of $2 million during the month of August. This was more than any other city comparable in size.

In 1946, the United States Hotel was demolished, and with it a pretty three acre park the U shaped structure had enclosed. The decision to suspend racing at Saratoga for the duration of World War II was a major blow to the hotel business at the spa. In 1943 the United States Hotel had fallen to the city for back taxes, and the lack of patronage was just more than the million dollar showplace could handle.

In 1951, a series of hearings were held in New York City with respect to organized crime. Headed by Estes Kefauver, the United States Senator from Tennessee launched an investigation of Saratoga Springs. Thomas E. Dewey, Governor of New York supported the investigation and ordered a grand jury to look into the activities. As a result Saratoga's casinos were closed and remained closed. This ended a virtually continuous run of public gaming since John Morrissey's arrival in 1861.

In 1952 at the close of the racing season, the Grand Union Hotel closed, thus joining the growing number of Saratoga's " has beens." Today, as we near the end of the century, Saratoga continues to host the August meet for the New York Racing Association. And, as part of Saratoga tradition, motel rates, restaurant prices and other retail prices escalate during the season.

Many residents of the city rent rooms in their homes, while others rent their homes for the entire season, and often the price is a five figure amount. There continues to be the many cocktail parties and other social events, including some that benefit certain charities. Saratoga's Broadway reflects the old and the new. The grounds on which the grand hotels once stood are now occupied by retail shops and restaurants. The Rip Van Dam and the Adelphi, two smaller hotels, remain open for business. Many of the old mansions and cottages still stand on North Broadway and along the quiet, tree shaded streets east and west of Broadway.

3. Lexington

I mentioned earlier that my interest in the Thoroughbred yearling developed as a result of my annual visits to the Fasig-Tipton
Saratoga sales. That interest also created for me a strong curiosity for
the state of Kentucky, in particular the city of Lexington.

I was able to satisfy that curiosity by traveling to Kentucky in
October of 1995. I found the area, situated in the East South Central
section of the United States, to be a beautiful part of this great land we
call America. Kentucky is known as the home of Thoroughbred horses
and traditional homes. It is bounded on the north by the Ohio River,
which separates it from Ohio, Indiana and Illinois. On the east it is
separated by West Virginia and Virginia, on the south by Tennessee
and the west by the Mississippi River. Kentucky, during the eighteenth
century claimed the attention of the East and also Europe. It had attracted great interest, due to it being a region temperate and fertile,
abounding in wildlife of many sorts. It was indeed a "promised land."
The pioneers abandoned the "Old World" for the Kentucky frontier
and beyond. Many viewed the break from the European past a wise
and deliberate choice, on the whole beneficial to the emigrants and to
the public.

Even after the frontier had been pushed far beyond the Mississippi, Kentucky was a compelling symbol; a time when the west as a
whole came to be regarded as a garden by prospering settlers. The con-
viction remained that "Old Kaintuck" was the "Garden of the West." In
1837, Count Francesco Arese, while touring the new nation stated; "The
most sincere and least bombastic Americans tell you that the country

47

around Lexington is the garden of the United States: the others tell you it is the garden of the world! In reality it is very beautiful, but in a positive, numerical way, a money beauty, in short an American beauty." There is a story told in a chapter from George Washington Ranck's book, "History of Lexington" that describes ancient Lexington.

In 1776, some venturesome hunters from Boonesborough had their curiosity excited by some stones they found in the woods, where Lexington now stands. The stones, when removed were found to be so placed to conceal the entrance to an ancient catacomb, formed in solid rock fifteen feet below the surface of the earth. They discovered that a gradual descent from the opening brought them to a passage four feet wide and seven feet high.

This led to a spacious apartment in which were numerous niches which they were amazed to find occupied by bodies which from their perfect state of preservation had evidently been embalmed. For six years succeeding this discovery the region in which the catacomb was located was visited by bands of raging Indians and avenging whites. During this period of blood and passion the catacomb, with its ancient mummies, probably the rarest remains of a forgotten era that man has ever seen, were well nigh swept out of existence. This ancient city which stood, where now is Lexington has vanished like a dream.

The first real settlers of Lexington were not the American Indians, as no Indian Nation has ever built walled cities defended by entrenchments or buried their dead in sepulchers hewn in the solid rock. Who were they? We don't know. They had no literature, and when they died they were utterly forgotten. They lived and labored, and died before Columbus had planted the standard old "Spain" upon the shores of a new world.

On June 7, 1769 Daniel Boone, the "Columbus of the Land" stood upon a lofty cliff which towered above a branch of the Kentucky River and gazed upon the "Italy of America." This frontiersman and Indian fighter, a conqueror of the wilderness first arrived in Kentucky in 1767. Boone and his army decided on the future for this dark and bloody ground.

In 1773 Boone was followed by a band of Virginia surveyors appointed by Lord Dunmore. Cabins were erected and corn was raised in the area, now called Harrodsburg. Boone built on the Kentucky River, the log fort and capital of the famous Transylvania Colony. In 1775, the first permanent and real settlement of Kentucky began. This event filled the Indians with rage —— to them the white men were invaders and robbers. They were determined to exterminate the white man, and regain every piece of soil.

General Robert McAfee in his history of the War of 1812 stated that Robert Patterson, Simon Kenton, Michael Stoner, John Haggin, John and Levi Todd took possession of the north side of the Kentucky River. The year was 1775. There were others, John Maxwell, Hugh Shannon, James Masterson, William McConnell, Isaac Grier and James Dunkin. They were the first white men to settle in what is now Lexington.

They searched for a name. York and Lancaster were two choices. The story of how "King George's" troops were dispatched from Boston on April 19, 1775 to seize the Americans at Concord—— and in fact shot them down like dogs at Lexington in Massachusetts Colony was fresh in their minds. The story of Lexington's christening, the historic fact of how she got her name, as romantic as the legend of the beautiful Princess "Pocahontas" is an incident far more interesting. It carries more truth than the fabulous one told of the founding of Rome.

So the hunters called the settlement "Lexington" after the memory of a bloody field hundreds of miles away. Some men later joined the Continental Army in an effort to avenge the minutemen who fell that day. Lexington was the name, but no settlement was effected until four years later. The summer of 1776 found no white man in all the length and breadth of the present Fayette County.

The American Revolution had now opened, Ticonderoga had been captured and the battle of Bunker Hill had been fought. One of the saddest tragedies of that eventful struggle had been enacted upon the Plains of Abraham. The Indians had enlisted on the side of England, and the northwestern tribes were not slow to act. They came to

Kentucky with the buds of spring. All of Fayette County was filled with roaming bands of angry "Shawanese" and "Cherokees." Any idea of dealing with the new settlement was abandoned by the white man.

Settlers were killed everyday. On July 14, 1776 one of Daniel Boone's daughters was captured, within rifle shot of Boonesborough, the fort built by Boone. Colonel Robert Patterson, born of Irish parents settled at Harrodsburg in 1776, and built a fort. In March of 1779, Patterson, a gallant Indian fighter was ordered from the fort at Harrodsburg to establish a garrison north of the Kentucky River. He took his 25 men and marched to the beautiful and fertile garden spot he had visited four years earlier. He erected a block house.

About that time immigrants were arriving in Lexington in increasing numbers, to get the benefit of settlement rights, under which Virginia guaranteed them a magnificent estate, which right was to cease in 1780. They built cabins and a fort, which was later to include an addition to the original construction. John Maxwell, born in Scotland in 1747 and John and Levi Todd settled around 1780. In 1781 Colonel John Todd made Lexington his permanent home. He was one of its most prominent citizens. He commanded the Lexington militia in the battle of the Blue Lick Springs, the last battle of the Revolution. He died at that time. The year was 1782.

The history of Lexington's education dates from the commencement of the city itself. The fort had its little school by 1780, taught by John McKinney. Transylvania Seminary was later located in Lexington. It was chartered by the legislature of Virginia. At the close of the Revolutionary War, the British and Indians ceased to annoy and distress the settlers.

The first trustees of the town at that time began to reserve ground for "Latin and English" schools. In 1787 Isaac Wilson of Philadelphia College established the Lexington grammar school. In 1798 Transylvania Seminary and its rival school, Kentucky Academy merged; the name being Transylvania University, Lexington. The first President was the Reverend James Moore, who bestowed the first degrees in 1802.

In 1782 the British House of Commons was encouraging a termination of the war against the American Colonies. In May of that year the second Board of Trustees of Lexington received a copy of the law passed by the Virginia Assembly at Richmond, incorporating Lexington. The law was entitled, "An act to establish a town at the courthouse in the county of Fayette."

On January 20, 1783 hostilities ceased between the armies of the United States and England. The news was received with great joy by the settlers in Fayette County. It did not bring with it security from the Indians. The settlers of Lexington were however, now encouraged to build cabins outside the walls of the fort. This allowed them to garden and other civilized things. By 1784 Lexington began to take appearance as a frontier village. It began a period in time when Lexington citizens developed and improved the area.

A dry goods store was opened by General James Wilkinson in 1784. The goods came from Philadelphia to Pittsburg by wagon, then by flat boat to Limestown and to Lexington by pack horses. The state of affairs in Lexington in 1785 may be inferred from a number of things. "Main Cross" Street, now Broadway was opened. The first tavern in Lexington opened at this time. It stood on West Main Street between Main Cross. The sign announcing the tavern read,

"Entertainment for man and beast by James Bray."

The early taverns were veritable old English Inns with quaint signs, smiling bonifaces and everything to match. Robert Megowan's tavern sign read,

"Sheaf of Wheat."

This was the second one built. It was a two story log house on Main Street between Upper and Limestone. Two other early taverns were "The Buffalo" and Kisers "Indian Queen," both known as houses of entertainment.

The "Taverns and Inns" of Kentucky were described as an out-growth of the times and modes of travel. It is written that stage coach travel in the Bluegrass would not have been so picturesque and color-ful, if it had not been for the part the taverns played in the accommoda-tion of travelers and towns folk.

Travel into central Kentucky during its formative period, the latter part of the eighteenth century, was not only by land but by boat down the Ohio River. During the Revolution and for sometime after-wards such travel was dangerous because of Indian attacks and floods and swift currents in river navigation. In addition, good boats were scarce and expensive, so a land route, though longer, was preferred by many of the early pioneers and settlers.

Toward the end of 1793 improvements were being made by private enterprises on the main trails and traces leading into the Blue-grass, converting them into "wagon roads" over which a wheeled ve-hicle might be drawn. On August 9, 1803, John Kennedy, a resident of Lexington announced he had started the first regular stage coach line in Kentucky. It would run from Lexington, by Winchester and Mt. Sterling to the Olympian Springs in Montgomery County, a distance of forty-seven miles.

In time with the opening of a stage line between Lexington and Frankfort the mail was transferred to the stage coach, and the post rider became an institution of the past. The coaches were home made and accommodated six to eight people. The passengers shared the in-terior with bulky merchandise, and were subject to a very uncomfort-able experience.

As time went on improvements to stage travel occurred, but toward the end of the nineteenth century the railroad began to replace the stage coach as a principal mode of travel. The last stage coach run from Lexington to Harrodsburg was completed on July 22, 1877. The taverns and inns remained a part of Lexington. Lexington had many taverns, described earlier as veritable old English Inns, with quaint signs, smiling bonifaces and everything to match. Anyone wishing to open and operate a tavern or inn made formal application to the board of magistrates with suitable surety for his good behavior and the peace and order of the establishment. Upon the fulfillment of the conditions, license was granted for one year, perhaps, reading as follows,

> "Tavern license granted
> John Postlethwait
> agreeable to law, upon
> his entering into bond
> with Joseph Hawkins as
> surety."

Judging from the large number of inns and taverns scattered throughout the Bluegrass, it is evident they played a very important part in the political and social life of the people. Many were the reasons that could be given to explain and justify attendance at the old time tavern. One was that often the only newspaper that came to the village was kept therein.

The first newspaper ever published west of the Allegheny mountains was established in Lexington in 1787 by John Bradford. It was called the "Kentucke Gazette," but the final "e" was changed to a "y". The paper was born of the necessities of the times. The want of a government independent of Virginia was universally felt, and the second convention that met in Danville in 1785 to discuss that subject resolved,

> "That to insure
> unanimity in the
> opinion of the people
> respecting the property
> of separating the
> district of Kentucky
> from Virginia and
> forming a separate
> state government and
> to give publicity
> to the proceedings
> of the convention."

John Bradford called on General Wilkinson, one of the committee and informed him that he would establish a paper if the convention would guaranty him the public patronage. The convention acceded and Bradford sent to Philadelphia for the necessary materials. He was encouraged by the people of Lexington to do this. He was given a lot free as long as he established his printing press in Lexington.

The center of the "Garden Spot" of Kentucky, justly famous the world over for its magnificent bloodstock was devoted to the turf while Lexington was scarcely a village. As early as 1787 the commons of Water Street was a favorite resort for horsemen. In August of 1789 the newspaper printed,

> "A purse race
> will take place
> at Lexington on
> the second
> Thursday in October,
> free for any horse,
> mare or gelding;
> weight for age
> agreeable to the
> rules of New Market
> (three mile heats)
> best two in three."

By 1802, races were in full blast in Lexington. In 1809 the Lexington Jockey Club was organized. It lasted until 1823. The first formal celebration of Independence Day in Lexington took place in 1788. While Kentucky was struggling for separate state sovereignty, the ruins of old confederation were lying all around her. The city of Cincinnati was settled by a company from Lexington. The original name for the settlement that occurred in 1788 was "Losantiville."

On June 1, 1792 after a long series of petitions, conventions, delegations to Virginia and acts of Virginia legislature, the U.S. Congress settled the matter by making Kentucky a state, the first beyond the Alleghenies. Dating back to 1584, Virginia had claimed Kentucky as part of the charter grant of that year.

On June 4, 1792 the first session of the Kentucky legislature commenced and the organization of the state government began. Early in the morning of that eventful day, the infant Capital of the new state presented a scene of unusual bustle and excitement. This was something the citizens of Kentucky had been waiting for and was destined to be an era in history, for on this day Isaac Shelby was to take the oath of office as governor of a commonwealth, then but three days old. The work of setting up the political machinery of the new state was beginning.

In 1793 the citizens of Lexington were upset as the state capital was moved from Lexington to Frankfort. This year also commenced the history of invention in Lexington, for at that time the first steamboat that ever plowed the waters of the world was invented. Edward West, a Virginian moved to Lexington in 1785 as a watchmaker. He had earlier built a steamboat on the "Seine." In 1796 Nathan Burrowes invented a machine to clean hemp.

In 1835 E. S. Noble invented a labor saving machine for the purpose of turning the bead on house guttering. Henry Clay, the great orator and statesman was born in the "Slashes" neighborhood of Hanover County Virginia on April 12, 1777. Clay immigrated to Lexington, Kentucky in 1797, shortly after obtaining his right to practice law. In 1803 he was elected to the Kentucky legislature and then in 1806 was named to fill an unexpired term in the U.S. Senate. Henry Clay later served as speaker of the Kentucky legislature, only to return to the U.S. Senate in 1810 to fill an unexpired term. In 1811, he was elected to the U.S. House of Representatives, where he served four terms as speaker.

For years Clay enjoyed the reputation as an eminent debater and platform orator. Henry Clay was a candidate for President in 1825, 1832 and 1844, but was defeated all three times. He returned to the U.S. Senate in 1849 and took the foremost part in formulating the bill known as the Compromise of 1850 or the Omnibus Bill. On account of this measure and various others he became known as the "Great Pacificator" and the "Great Compromiser." Henry Clay died June 29, 1852 with more than 40 years of public life to his credit.

Lexington was at the zenith of her commercial prosperity in 1810. Since 1800 her growth had been so rapid her population tripled. At that time the population in Lexington was 8,000 and Fayette County was more than 21,000. There were many commercial establishments lining the streets of Lexington; paper mills, tobacco factories, cabinet shops, powder mills, nail factories and at least one mustard factory. Then came a decline in trade and population that lasted until around 1820. The opening of steam navigation on the Ohio River revolutionized the trade channels of the western part of the country. In 1816 Lexington was known as one of the most fashionable cities in the west.

The Civil War brought a great deal of change to Lexington and the entire state of Kentucky. The state was divided in sentiment. Unable to remain neutral or to escape the conflict, Kentucky did not secede from the Union, but Kentuckians joined both sides of the struggle. Confederate and Union forces invaded the state, fighting battles at Mills Springs, Richmond and Perryville. Union troops gained control in 1862 and held the state until the war ended in 1865.

After the Civil War, Kentucky was spared the turmoil of Reconstruction, since it did not need to seek readmission to the Union; but many adjustments had to be made when slavery was abolished. By 1870 large scale production of coal was a big source of economic expansion for Kentucky. In addition, the steel business was also developing, in particular at Ashland.

The first half of the nineteenth century was a time when breeding of horses became more and more popular in the state of Kentucky. By 1865 the reputation of Kentucky-bred horses was firmly established. Earlier, many well known sporting journals like the "American Turf Register" had covered the activity extensively. This resulted in widespread recognition, both on the national and international scene. Some of the articles carried detailed descriptions of races, bloodlines and horse owners and breeders.

Because of the Civil War the horse world in Kentucky underwent many changes. In the earlier days the southern market for Kentucky livestock was more focused on farm work animals rather than on sporting horses. Up north the emergence of a national industry created a new and affluent type of American capitalistic aristocracy. This included the breeding and racing of superior horses.

After 1875 the Kentucky horse world assumed social and economic dimensions undreamed of in previous decades. Many Kentucky livestock breeders recouped Civil War and postwar depression losses by breeding horses for a rapidly expanding national market.

Prior to the Civil War, racing centers in the south were not yet overshadowed by the "Big Apple." Yet, the fact is that from the earliest days the breeding and racing business in Kentucky were linked with the major racing courses and sportsmen of New York. This is still true today, when many of the farms and horses grazing in their fields in the Bluegrass are the property of businessmen from New York and elsewhere.

Racing in Kentucky today is centered in Lexington and Louisville. In 1933 the Kentucky Association Track in Lexington, after more than a century of racing was replaced by Keeneland. The Keeneland Track was built by a group of Bluegrass horsemen, mindful of the desirability of having a place to train, race and sell Thoroughbreds. The most important races at Keeneland are the Blue Grass Stakes, which is the final major prep for the Kentucky Derby and the Spinster Stakes in the fall.

Lexington is known as the horse capital of the world, due to the extent of the breeding business carried on there. As a state, Kentucky enjoys a reputation for producing a very high percentage of all North American bred-stakes winners. In 1985 there were 130 horse farms in Fayette County, the greatest concentration being an area west of Lexington, stretching across the northern part of the county to the east of Lexington.

In addition to the famous Thoroughbreds, dozens of other breeds of horses are raised in Lexington.

Four such breeds are: Standardbred, Morgan, Arabian and Miniatures. The land for Calumet Farm was purchased in 1924 by William Monroe Wright, founder of the Calumet Baking Powder Company of Chicago. In 1931 Warren Wright inherited Calumet Farm after the death of his father and switched from the Standardbred business to Thoroughbreds. Over the years Calumet has produced many outstanding horses, including "Triple Crown" winners , Whirlaway and Citation. The greatest stallion to stand at Calumet was Bull Lea, with 58 stakes winners to his credit.

Darby Dan Farm produced Chateaugay, the winner of the 1963 Kentucky Derby and Belmont. Proud Clarion, the winner of the 1967 Derby was also a product of Darby Dan Farm. Graustark, His Majesty and Roberto were three stallions that stood at Darby Dan Farm.

Spendthrift Farm, a 3000 acre spread enjoys the reputation as one of the worlds foremost commercial Thoroughbred breeding establishments. The farm has been owned and managed by the Combs family for many years. For a collective period, 1968-1978 Spendthrift was the nations leading breeder of nonrestricted stakes winners. The list of great stallions that have stood at Spendthrift includes Gallant Man, Majestic Prince, Raise a Native, Exclusive Native and Wajima. In addition, "Triple Crown" winners Seattle Slew and Affirmed stood for a time at Spendthrift.

Spendthrift Farm began in 1937 when Leslie Combs II purchased 127 acres from the estate of Hector Lewis. General Leslie Combs, great grandfather of the farm's founder was one of the charter members of the Kentucky Association for the Improvement of Breeds of Stock. The many farms surrounding the greater Lexington area in Fayette County and neighboring Bourbon County are a major factor in Kentucky's economy. Perhaps the most famous horse farm in Bourbon County is Claiborne Farm. Claiborne is located in Paris Kentucky, the place where Secretariat began his stallion days back in 1974.

Bold Ruler, the sire of Secretariat was foaled at Claiborne in 1954. His descendants dominated the Kentucky Derby in the 1970s. Seven of them won the Derby and two of them won the Triple Crown: Dust Commander, Secretariat, Cannonade, Foolish Pleasure, Bold Forbes, Seattle Slew and Spectacular Bid. Wajima, champion three year old in 1975, was another brilliant son.

The city of Lexington has enjoyed a tremendous amount of economic contribution from the horse farms, especially during the twentieth century. The scenic routes, such as Old Frankfort Pike, Paris Pike and Versailles Road offer a breathtaking view, not only for visitors but for the local people too. The large farms, with beautiful homes, fancy barns and yearlings grazing in a pasture lined with white fence, is a sight one will never forget.

As our great country prepares for the next century, Lexington is said to be a city where,

> some of the wealthiest
> residents are horses.
>
> frequent visitors include
> queens, counts and sheiks.
>
> people have to ask what
> color the grass is.
>
> hospitality is a word
> that still has meaning.

The Keeneland Racecourse is to Lexington what the Saratoga Racecourse is to Saratoga Springs. As recent as 1995 Lexington was home to 13 of the 18 living Kentucky Derby winners. The 1976 winner, Bold Forbes resides in the Hall of Champions at the Kentucky Horse Park. Man o' War, the big red stallion considered to be the greatest race horse of all time stands forever in bronze at the entrance to the park.

Lexington is also the "Wildcat" capital of the world and home of the University of Kentucky, founded in 1865. There are colleges of agriculture, arts and sciences, journalism, education, engineering, law and medicine. In addition, the university has an outstanding athletic program.

For sure Lexington has something for everyone. There is horse racing, golf, beautiful parks, museums, shopping, great hotel accommodations and many fine restaurants. You name it —— it is here.

After visiting Lexington in 1995, I left with a good feeling for the area. I had learned a great deal about the area, and fully appreciated what the horse business has done for Lexington and the entire state of Kentucky. I know there is a great deal of competition in the breeding business, and with our changing world and new technology, other states can offer what the Bluegrass can offer.

I hope and pray that the state of Kentucky will always lead the way in the breeding of Thoroughbreds, and that Lexington plays a major role.

As they say in the "Visitors Guide":

"Lexington is anything but typical."

Part II

The Other Side

More of Everything Else

4.   The Beginning

As I was writing the first part of my book I was always conscious of how I would move my story to what I refer to as the "horse side" of the writing. The side that reflects on the careers of some bargain yearlings that had a "claim to fame" in the sport of Thoroughbred racing.

I also wanted to learn more about the breeding side of the business and what it takes to bring a Thoroughbred prospect to the auction block. From a training standpoint the yearling year is one of vast importance. The manners and gentleness developed during the second year of life will be remembered for the duration of the animal's existence. It is therefore imperative that the yearling has a good start. A great deal of time is required for dealing with a yearling, especially in the area of proper feeding with an abundance of supervised exercise.

I have learned that writing a book that combines real life experiences with a part of history is a great way to stretch an interest in something to the point it becomes knowledge.

The transition begins with some history of "Thoroughbred Racing in America," and a look at the breeding side of the business.

The Thoroughbred industry continues to be very strong in the United States. More than half of all the Thoroughbred horses in the world are foaled in America. The Thoroughbred establishment, including breeding farms, livestock and racecourses represents a multi billion dollar industry. In 1995 some 35 million fans wagered $12.5 billion.

For the purpose of this writing I focus on Thoroughbred racing in America. The top breeders and stable owners in the United States produce and race animals of a quality comparable to any that can be found in any other part of the world. In the industry there are many sprinters that can go a mile or less, that are foaled. Some feel the true test of a champion is the horse that can go the distance from a mile and a quarter to two miles. History has shown that many horses, have won one or two legs of the triple crown only to be beat in the final event, the "Belmont," with a distance of one and one half miles. Horsemen know that it is far more predictable to breed for short speed than it is for stamina over the longer routes.

The first horse races on American soil were held on the rutted dirt streets of Colonial towns. It actually can be traced back to the early years of the seventeenth century. In the middle, and continuing to the late seventeenth century, the prosperous planters of Virginia, Maryland and South Carolina began importing "horses of the blood" from England.

Unfortunately, the good horses were unsuited to the mad pace of the quarter mile race, in which horses were sent off from a rearing, plunging start at the tap of a drum or a musket shot. At that point the colonists discovered that by crossing the good English horses with the tough Chickasaw ponies they acquired by bartering with the Indians, they could develop a strain of animals with blinding start up speed required in racing. This breed of horse lost popularity around 1700 — — at which time they began to find there way to the American West, where they regained popularity for qualities such as agility, ruggedness and "stock sense" needed by the American cowboy to handle the bands of cattle that roamed the great plains. Today, this breed is part of the Quarter Horse family.

The first formal race track in America was believed to have been located at a place called Salisbury Plain, in the vicinity of Garden City Long Island, near the spot where Belmont is now located. It was founded by Colonel Richard Nicolls, Colonial Governor of New York. The track opened in 1665 and was called Newmarket after a track in England.

The American Revolution began in 1776, when the colonies declared their independence of Great Britan. It ended with the surrender of Cornwallis at Yorktown in 1781. Following the war, the citizens of the new nation were quick to bring racing back. Between 1784 and 1798 four English stallions were imported from England and from these sires were developed bloodlines, not only of great importance in early American Thoroughbred breeding, but still to be found in the pedigrees of many of the best American horses.

I never realized it but according to my research George Washington and Thomas Jefferson were prominent figures in racing during the period of time preceeding the war.

As time passed, American breeders went back to the well for new infusions of English blood. A sire named Glencoe, purchased by James Jackson, a native of Ireland in 1838 was at that time the leading sire imported from England. The states of Virginia and Maryland led the parade of states to expand breeding and racing. Subsequently, New York, in particular New York City entered the arena in a big way.

By 1823 there was mounting evidence of a rivalry brewing between North and South. In the years leading up to the American Civil War racing expanded rapidly in the United States. The tracks up to that point were no more than an oval racing strip enclosed by rails. As new tracks were built, they were more elaborate with grandstands and concession facilities. In addition, public betting through bookmakers became part of the scene.

At the close of the pre-Civil War period, the cities of New York, Baltimore, Cincinnati, New Orleans, Chicago, Charleston and St. Louis all engaged in racing activities. In the state of California, the great gold rush was good for the small tracks that were operating there. It was clear that Thoroughbred racing had a future, especially in the big cities.

The years that followed the Civil War period saw a change for the industry. Many breeders previously based in Virginia relocated to the state of Kentucky. The state of Kentucky had been spared much of the devastation caused by the war. To this day Kentucky continues to be a leader in the quality and quantity of Thoroughbreds raised.

As the twentieth century draws to a close, Kentucky, Virginia, Maryland, California,Florida and New York remain very active states for breeding Thoroughbreds.

In 1864 Old Saratoga opened its gates for the first time. Following Saratoga's opening was Pimlico in 1870, the Fair Grounds at New Orleans in 1872 and Churchill Downs at Louisville, Kentucky in 1875. The Kentucky Derby, America's most famous race is run at Churchill Downs.

Saratoga features the running of the Travers, the oldest stake race in America for three year olds. As these four tracks gained popularity, racing in states like Georgia, Alabama, Tennessee, Virginia and the Carolinas all but vanished.

The post Civil War period brought a change in the style of racing. The running of a race in "heats" was abandoned. The jockeys, often considered not an important part of racing came to the fore as sort of hero (if he won) and a villain (if he lost). The three greatest American jockeys at that time were Tod Sloan, Danny Maher and Isaac "Ike" Murphy. Murphy, a well known black rider won an amazing 616 races out of a recorded 1400 mounts. He made a lot of money and retired at age 37, only to die of pneumonia soon after.

In the latter part of the nineteenth century four very important races were established. The Travers, as mentioned was first run in 1864 at Saratoga, and continues to be run each August at the "Spa." The Belmont was first contested in 1867. The running of the Preakness began in 1873, followed by the Kentucky Derby two years later. Maryland's Dixie Handicap and New York's Jerome Stakes for three year olds were among other American races originating during the immediate post war period.

The "golden age" of American racing was a period of time between 1865 and 1914, the start of World War I. It was a time for great animals and good racing. Unfortunately, these times also presented a dark side for the sport —— doping animals, fixing races and the substitution of horse identity. That is, horses racing under other names than their own. In 1894, the "Jockey Club" was established, which brought organization and a solid level of responsibility back to Thoroughbred racing.

The evil practices that were present for a time seriously damaged the horse racing industry. The story of how racing in the United States started its painful comeback goes back to the 1908 running of the Kentucky Derby. At this time the city fathers in Louisville were also feeling some of the antiracing pressure that had been effective in other areas. An obscure "blue law," which forbade track side bookmaking was suddenly brought to the light and the city government announced that it would be enforced.

Matt Winn, the manager of Churchill Downs reacted by resurrecting an idea he had failed with a few years earlier. The idea that had not proved popular with the betting crowd was the use of French totalisator machines. The reintroduction of these machines, through which the public establishes its own odds according to amounts bet on each horse in a race made sense at this time. The machines took the place of the track side bookmakers, and saved the Derby. In time the use of pari-mutuel machines became widespread, and brought other changes.

The use of mechanical odds-makers to record each sum wagered made it easy for the lawmakers to perceive that a regular percentage could be deducted from each betting pool. The result, licensing requirements and a lucrative revenue stream for the states. In addition, as time passed, the increased amount of accountability and organized practices made it difficult for the big time gamblers to beat the system. Thoroughbred racing in America bounced back.

As the curtain comes down on the twentieth century, it will have been a great 100 years for Thoroughbred racing. Among the countless thousands of great racehorses, eleven emerged as "Triple Crown" winners.

They were:

Sir Barton	1919
Gallant Fox	1930
Omaha	1935
War Admiral	1937
Whirlaway	1941
Count Fleet	1943
Assault	1946
Citation	1948
Secretariat	1973
Seattle Slew	1977
Affirmed	1978

However, despite all the great things that have happened in Thoroughbred racing, the industry is not without problems. In particular one area that is being scrutinized is the media of television. Since 1990 ratings for horse racing on TV have decreased. In 1995, the Kentucky Derby earned a rating of 6.0 compared to 7.5 in 1994 and 10.1 in 1990. Industry marketing people feel the sport has to be made entertainable.

Sports such as professional golf, football, basketball and even NASCAR racing have experienced a great deal of success from TV exposure. The key to success is to obtain sponsors and make the sport attractive to them. A change in the way the industry does business is inevitable. My response to that —— there is no business out there that has not experienced change, especially during the last few years.

Some tracks have already introduced new ideas, the use of signage along the finish line and tote boards. The people responsible for finding ways to attract people to racing agree the sport has to be willing to display sponsor names. A sponsor agrees to being a sponsor for the purpose of getting their products and/or images seen on national TV. In today's world there is a tremendous amount of competition for the "pleasure dollars." Tracks have introduced family days, happy hours and other special events. At Saratoga '"T Shirt" day draws a lot of people. Some pay five or ten times just to get an equal number of T Shirts. Oh well!

A 1995 survey conducted by The Blood-Horse magazine disclosed that advertising and promotion budgets ranged from $500,000 at Aksarben to $5 million at the New York Racing Association. Some marketing people feel the best way to promote racing is to band together to form a national ad campaign. In my mind Thoroughbred racing is no different than many other industries. Race tracks operate in geographical locations, some that are economically sound and others that are not.

The racing industry will always have the loyal die-hard fans. It is important to attract new people. This fact is not unique to horse racing. In my mind the "powers that be" will find a way and the sport will survive.

My interest in the Fasig-Tipton annual yearling sales began around 1969. We would always vacation in Saratoga the second and third week of racing. These were the two biggest weeks for the meet, with the yearling sales followed by the historic running of the Travers Stakes the third Saturday.

I loved to walk around the Fasig-Tipton grounds on East Avenue during the day and watch interested buyers studying the animals as they were paraded back and forth. In those days the sales were held Tuesday, Wednesday, Thursday and Friday of the second week of racing. I can still see Humphrey S. Finney the late Chairman of Fasig-Tipton walking around the grounds with his walking stick and spectacles drawn down over his nose. Mr. Finney was in my mind a very interesting person, a man who began his career with horses at the age of 18 upon arrival in New York from his home in Manchester, England. I am very familiar with the Manchester area, having served as a flying crew member for the United States Air Force, back in the 1950's. Burtonwood Air Force Base in Manchester was a scheduled cargo drop for us.

I would marvel at the beauty of these yearlings, and the manner in which they were groomed. And then to return for the evening sale, I watched in total amazement over the prices they would bring. I visualized in my mind the amount of work it must have required to bring a new foal to the yearling stage and then to the point of sale at Saratoga or Keeneland.

In July of 1996 I traveled to Milfer Farm in Unadilla, New York to catch a glimpse at a first class breeding farm. The farm is owned by Dr. Jonathan H.F. Davis, a prominent veterinarian. I was able to spend time with Joel Reach, the farm manager. He was kind enough to take me on a tour of the farm. During that part of my visit, I was introduced to two popular stallions — "Spectacular Bid", and "Cure The Blues."

Joel, a graduate of Alfred State University supervises a staff of 18 and lives on the 1200 acre main farm with his son. At the time of my visit, there were four stallions and 100 broodmares in residence. I enjoyed my afternoon on the farm, grasping an opportunity to satisfy my curiosity concerning the scientific nature of the business.

Those in the business of breeding Thoroughbred race horses believe the selection of a stallion is of primary importance. Perhaps even more imperative is the mares side of the pedigree, as the mare is responsible for 60 per cent of the quality of the foal. It is important to avoid the breeding of inferior females, one of poor conformation or one with an inheritable weakness. Joel agreed that a breeder knows that at times a highly desirable mare can produce a foal that will not perform well for the owner. It is not uncommon for a desirable mare of excellent conformation and bloodlines bred to a good Thoroughbred stallion to produce a foal with bad "hocks." Hocks being the ever important "tarsal joint" found in the hind leg of a horse.

And, conversely of course a mare considered to be "common" of head and neck can produce a champion. For sure, according to Joel, it is a risky business but for him enjoyable. I talked to several people engaged in the breeding business and the consensus seems to be that it is dangerous to breed a mare that has obvious defects. The exception seems to be a case where the defect is the result of an injury. In the selection process it is important to examine the mares foals as well as the mare herself.

The quality mare should stand not less than sixteen hands, be of good bone and well barreled. She should milk well so as to give her foal a good start in life. An average mare will produce but four foals in five years. A stallion will serve upward of forty mares in one season. Therefore, one or two broodmares in the group is tolerable but a bad stallion is not good.

I met Tony Cissell, stallion manager for Calumet Farms on August 7, 1996. Tony's background was very similar to Joel Reach's, some sixteen years in the business, four with Calumet. I shared with Tony some of my experiences during my stay in Lexington. Calumet Farm is located on Versailles Road in Lexington very close to the Keeneland Racecourse.

Both Tony and Joel agree that it is very important to examine a stallion carefully, as part of the normal selection process. In addition, it is beneficial to select a stallion that has had previous experience. The actual breeding or mating of the mares to the stallion is a process that begins with a commitment to certain principles.

The key to success is the female reaching the point of conception. Without that a breeder is merely running a boarding house for stallions and wayward mares. A smart breeder will rely on good advice from an experienced veterinarian — that staying as close to nature as possible will result in a greater number of foals reaching maturity.

Stallions should be stabled in large roomy box stalls with doors leading to their individual paddocks never closed. The barns are never heated. It is extremely important for a stallion to exercise at least twice a week and be with no more than five or six mares a week. The normal breeding season is from February to July. During that time a stallion is fed six quarts of grain three times each day, with no allowance for growing soft or fat.

A normal balanced diet would consist of five parts rolled oats, three parts rolled barley, two parts wheat bran, one part linseed meal and during the cold months, one part of cracked corn. To this can be added six carrots split lengthwise. If the stallion becomes sluggish, two to three eggs may be added to each feed, as well as a modest amount of yeast.

It is critical for the breeder to be sure the mare being taken to a stallion is in season. If there is any doubt, the mare should not be brought in. The stallion should not frighten the mare. He should be disciplined and not rush the mare. After the breeding the stallion is immediately returned to his stall. The mare is washed and turned out to pasture with the foal for a two week period.

I found all this information extremely interesting and from my conversations with people closely connected to the breeding business, a great deal of love for their work. I visited with Ron Green, owner of Green Willow Farm in Westminster, Maryland during my stay in Saratoga in August of 1996. Ron has been in the industry for 25 years. Prior to entering the world of Thoroughbreds, he worked with dairy cattle. He assured me it is a good business to be in, but you have to love it. In talking with Ron, I sensed a real love for the challenge of getting a yearling to the sales at Keeneland and Saratoga. He has been coming to Saratoga for six years.

At the time of our visit, Ron had eight stallions and 150 broodmares in residence on his 850 acre farm. I learned that a new foal is permitted to get to its feet unassisted. It is normal for foals to rise to their feet and nurse within the first hour of life. Often, it will take two or three attempts before the foal is able to remain standing.

After the foal has nursed for the first time, the stall is cleaned out and fresh bedding is spread. Both the mare and foal should be given as much privacy as possible. Some breeders place the mare and foal in a small paddock adjacent to the larger pastures that contain the balance of the band. This gives the new foal a chance to visit over the fence and become accustomed to the remainder of the band before they are all turned out together.

A foal should be handled as soon after birth as possible to assure gentleness and confidence in man. As weaning time approaches many breeders find it advisable to add dry skim milk to the foal ration. This is increased from a quarter pound to one or two pounds daily at the time of weaning. For the balance of the foal year (after weaning) the foals do nothing but eat, sleep and exercise. In cold areas, such as winter at Milfer Farm, foals are barned during that time of year.

In warm weather the foals are allowed to run in small pastures and given all the hay they can clean up. Joel Reach informed me that they make all their own hay at Milfer. Joel also shared with me that when a yearling is being readied for auction they are protected from the danger of sunburn. It never occurred to me that a horse could get sunburned.

At the age of 14 - 15 months a yearling is brought in from the paddock and assigned a stall in the training barn. They are groomed daily, with caution when rubbing their ears, and handling their heads. This is so they will not object to the application of the head stall later on.

The schooling of yearlings begins when they have become accustomed to being barned. This includes being comfortable tied in their stalls and allowing people to work around them. During the yearling year the animal is allowed to spend a lot of time in the pasture. This is a time when there will be considerable growing, and every possible feeding opportunity is important. From a feeding standpoint, the yearling year is the most important of the animals lifetime.

I certainly feel a lot smarter with respect to the finer points of breeding, but not confident enough to recognize a future winner out of the many yearlings that enter the ring at Keeneland and Saratoga. Tony Cissell of Calumet referred to the risk side of the business as being like the "NBA" draft. A game of chance. I laughed at that comment. Tony, a former student at the University of Kentucky and I went off on a tangent at that point with some conversation about the Syracuse - Kentucky final game of the 1996 NCAA basketball tournament. We both agreed that it was a great game —— only my team lost.

In buying Thoroughbred yearlings, sometimes you're right and sometimes you're wrong. Many great racehorses have had physical deformities or deficiencies which they were able to overcome.

I asked Ron Green and Tony Cissell if they could give me kind of a "gut" reason why Leroy Jolley purchased Foolish Pleasure back in 1973 when everyone else walked away from the colt. The answer to my question, though not with the same choice of words was almost identical. They both felt that Jolley may have seen a characteristic in the colt that was similar to another horse he may have trained with good results. That made sense to me.

In buying a yearling, the knowledgeable person starts with the pedigree. In the sales catalogue, the buyer should look for the ones with the most racing quality close up. If you go back far enough, it is likely you would find that every horse has ancestors that have won great races. A smart person also recognizes that blood lines may deteriorate or improve from generation to generation.

The late Humphrey S. Finney claimed the first things to look for in a pedigree as being: a stallion that is a proven sire, or a top class young racehorse from a proven family who can be expected to be a good sire; and a dam that was either a first class race mare, or has been a producer of high class racehorses. Further, when a yearling was brought out for inspection Finney looked to see if he came out smartly or like a snail. Finney always observed if the animal acted mean or nervous and the general impression provided.

The yearlings walk was important to Finney, if it was poor he felt the horse would not run well either. Ideally, in his mind the animal should have come straight at you, neither turning his feet out nor in. The consensus of the people I talked to agreed with a statement from Finney's book "Fair Exchange."

Anyone going into the horse business, either breeding or racing, needs money, intelligence and luck. A combination of any two isn't bad, but having all three is best.

In the late 1970s and to the mid 1980s, the multimillion-dollar stallion syndications sale of shares in a horse's breeding rights after becoming a winner, reached extremely high levels. At that time Arab oil sheiks, Texas oil barons, Wall Street speculators bid as much as $13 million for an untried yearling.

And, as mentioned it is not that easy to pick a winner out of the many yearlings led into the ring at Keeneland and Saratoga. In 1973 Secretariat became the first triple crown winner since Citation in 1948. In 1975 as a stallion, Secretariat set the trend for what would become an "era" of escalating prices.

A cool market analyst might have urged caution about Secretariat as a sire. In the breeding business, those in the know agree that matching a sire with a dam who will compensate for each others deficiencies and combine their strengths leads to success ——— usually. With Secretariat, there were no such deficiencies or personality quirks to compensate for. Breeders simply sent their best bred, best producing mares to produce winners.

The mares breeders sent to Secretariat, his first year as stud, were probably the strongest group ever assembled for a stallion. Most of them were accomplished both as race mares and as producers of top horses. Among them were mares that foaled Northern Dancer, Dahlia, Majestic Light, Arts and Letters and Reviewer. In time as foals were produced, it became obvious to the interested breeders that the foals could have been sired by any of the other stallions at Claiborne Farm.

In the fall of 1975, some of Secretariat's first foals were put up for auction as weanlings. In the horse game, weanlings sell for less than yearlings, since they are less developed and show fewer signs of possible talent. The weanling market is more speculative, at times buyers purchase with the idea of reselling as a yearling for a profit. In 1976 the select yearling sales at Keeneland and Saratoga were exciting. Amid an atmosphere of "grandeur," ten Secretariat yearlings consigned to the auctions broke every possible record. Seven sold at Keeneland for $2.61 million and the remaining three brought a flat million at Saratoga. I was at the sale on August 11, 1976 when hip number 87, a colt sold for $275,000. The following night August 12, 1976 hip number 156, a filly sold for $175,000 and number 193, a colt was purchased for $550,000. The total record average of $371,000 was almost double the $190,000 share cost for the great horse.

The top price paid for a yearling from the first crop of Secretariat foals was $1.5 million by John Sikura, a Canadian horseman. Without question, Secretariat will go down in history as a great horse on the track but less than spectacular as a sire. In defense of that, the world of Thoroughbred racing has to agree that Secretariat's potential rather than performance revolutionized the breeding industry.

From that point, additional million dollar yearlings began to surface. In 1978 one yearling sold for $1.3 million. In 1979 five went for between $1 million and $1.6 million. In 1980, there were five sales in excess of $1 million topped out at $1.7 million. In 1981, there were 13 million dollar yearlings— three sold for more than $2.9 million each. A new record of $3.5 million was established that year. And then came 1982, when 21 yearlings sold for more than a million dollars, with another new record — $4.25 million.

This gets better, how about hip number 308 at the 1983 Keeneland sale. The price paid was $10.2 million, a new record. Wow! The afternoon of July 23, 1985 proved exciting for those in attendance at the Keeneland sale. A bay colt, number 215 in the catalogue, sold for $13.1 million. The colt was the property of Warner Jones and his pedigree read —by Nijinsky out of My Charmer, by Poker. Nijinsky, horse of the year-in Europe and a leading sire, the son of Northern Dancer. The bidding was hot and heavy for an extended period of time. At the $7 million mark, the battle was down to two bidders. A group representing Robert Sangster, heir to a Liverpool England soccer betting operation was one of the two. The other was Wayne Lucas, bidding on behalf of Eugene V. Klein, former owner of the San Diego Chargers and Texas oilman L. R. French. The bidding continued, exceeding the previous record of $10.2 million until the gavel was silenced at $13.1 million. The Sangster group had won.

That amount of money is mind boggling, almost beyond my comprehension. I believe this is why I hold in high regard the many yearlings that have sold "cheap" only to go on to accomplish great victories. In the preface, I referred to Foolish Pleasure as the yearling sale that inspired me to write this book. When I visited Lexington, Kentucky in late 1995 my primary purpose was to do some research at the Keeneland Library. There I selected Spectacular Bid, Seattle Slew and Northern Dancer as three additional bargain yearlings to write about. As there were many others to choose from, I will include some of those not chosen in the final pages of the writing.

Foolish Pleasure

Member - National Thoroughbred Racing Hall of Fame
Saratoga Springs, N.Y.

5.   Foolish Pleasure

The day was August 7, 1973, a typical August day in Saratoga. Margie and I together with our daughters, Ann and Julie had arrived the previous Saturday for our annual summer visit.

My recollection of the events of the day were that we had gone swimming at the "Peerless" pool over in the state park during the afternoon. Then, on the way back to 77 White Street, we stopped at a vegetable stand on Route 9 for some fresh picked "corn on the cob" for dinner that night with Margie's dad. Her father was a widower, and he always looked forward to our visits.

Following dinner and cleaning up the dishes, Margie and her dad sat on the big front porch to enjoy an evening of conversation. Ann and Julie scooted across the street to play with the Orrill children. At about 8 P.M. I walked over to Union Avenue, directly behind 77 White Street and then over to the Fasig-Tipton facility on East Avenue, just a few blocks away. I never dreamed that a colt that would sell toward the end of the sale that night would inspire me to write a book some twenty - two years later. But, that is exactly what happened!

The colt, listed as hip number 53 in the catalogue was a March 23, 1972 foal. A Florida Bred, product of Waldemar Farms Inc. His Sire was What A Pleasure, a stakes winner, the son of Bold Ruler. Bold Ruler was also the sire of Secretariat. The dam, Fool-Me-Not was sired by Tom Fool, sire of Tim Tam, winner of the 1958 Kentucky Derby and Preakness. The pedigree was good.

The horsemen at the Saratoga auction that summer spotted the splayfooted yearling. "He toes out," they said and moved on to other yearlings. That is except for LeRoy Jolley, who liked the colt's strong body and widely spaced eyes. So the night of the sale, Jolley, acting on behalf of John Greer of Knoxville, Tennessee purchased the horse for $20,000. Mr. Greer was part owner of Ridan, a horse that Jolley had trained. Ridan was a third place finisher in the 1962 Derby. Later that year Ridan lost by an "inch" in the Travers to Jaipur. Many say that race was one of the greatest ever.

Moody Jolley, LeRoy's father, a trainer for more than fifty years felt good about a yearling that resembled a successful ancestor. He described the colt purchased by his son as a dead ringer for Tom Fool —— a quick learner. The colt would be named Foolish Pleasure, and being out of a daughter of Tom Fool was an enhancement to the pedigree.

Tom Fool, elected to the National Thoroughbred Racing Hall of Fame in 1960 was a champion at two and a good runner at three. His real claim to fame came as a stallion. At the completion of his racing career at four, he retired to Greentree Stud, near Lexington. In addition to Tim Tam, he sired more than 30 added money winners, including Buckpasser, Weatherwise, Jester and Tompion. Not bad! Interesting enough, when Foolish Pleasure first retired to Greentree, his assigned stall was one that Tom Fool once occupied. Another compact bay with a wide forehead and intelligent eye. Another that had combat in his heart.

I am grateful to Foolish Pleasure for creating in me the desire to write this book. The fact that I attended the yearling sales in Saratoga for many years afforded me the opportunity to select any number of Thoroughbreds to write about. I believe my sensitivity for a young horse that many found to be of little value; and then to reflect on his many great accomplishments is my answer. The answer to my own question. I really needed something to take this book beyond just a book that expressed my love for the city of Saratoga. Foolish Pleasure did that for me.

The career of Foolish Pleasure on the track was an exciting one, starting as a two year old, followed by success at three and at four. As a two year old he was unbeaten in seven races. The biggest thrill for John Greer that year was the colt's runaway triumph in the Champagne Stakes. Following that, Foolish Pleasure was rested, allowing for further maturity, prior to racing as a three year old.

As the year 1975 began to unfold, so did the career of Foolish Pleasure, the very popular three year old, that had sold as a bargain at Saratoga in 1973. By the third week in April he had extended his races to 11 with 10 wins, including the Wood Memorial at Aqueduct. His only defeat was in the Florida Derby at Gulfstream. He finished third behind Prince Thou Art and Sylvan Place.

It was time to prepare Foolish Pleasure for the Triple Crown of racing: The Kentucky Derby on May 3; the Preakness at Pimlico on May 17; the Belmont on June 7.

In the Kentucky Derby, the son of What A Pleasure came from far off the pace to win the 101st running. After the first quartermile, he led only four horses in the fifteen horse field. At the wire he was 1 3/4 lengths in front. Avatar was second followed by Diabolo. Prince Thou Art and Sylvan Place, the two horses that had finished in front of Foolish Pleasure in his only defeat, came in sixth and eighth respectively. The attendance was 113,324 and the handle was $3.3 million.

LeRoy Jolley, in an interview following the race was asked if he would compare his horse with Secretariat. Jolley replied, "Secretariat is the greatest horse I ever saw and Foolish Pleasure is the greatest horse I ever had. It's tough to compare the two but Foolish Pleasure has done everything we've asked of him."

Foolish Pleasure, with his victories in the Flamingo and the Wood Memorial, two important prep races for the Derby overcame a hex that had been felt by five previous contenders for the Kentucky crown jewel. Nashua, victorious in the two prep races in 1955 finished second in the Kentucky Derby. In 1944, Stir Up won both earlier events, only to come in third at Louisville. The others weren't even in the money.

Foolish Pleasure became the third Florida Bred to win the Kentucky Derby. The first was Needles in 1956 and the second was Carry Back, with John Sellers in the saddle in 1961. Foolish Pleasure ran in the Preakness and in the Belmont. He was beat by Master Derby in the Preakness. In the Belmont, the Derby winner battled Avatar the entire mile and a half, losing at the wire. Avatar won in 2:28 1/5. Following the Belmont that year, several tracks were seeking to promote a match race for Ruffian, the champion three year old filly.

In two short seasons Ruffian was hailed as the greatest Thoroughbred filly of all time. Unbeaten in her first ten starts, she had shattered one record after another; dazzling the crowds with her beauty and brilliant speed.

At one time a three horse race was being considered, with the participants being Ruffian, Foolish Pleasure and Master Derby, the Preakness winner. LeRoy Jolley was not in favor of this idea. The race would be awarded to Belmont Park, under the supervision of the New York Racing Association. The NYRA paid Master Derby's owner $50,000 from the $400,000 purse (in advance) for not running Master Derby. That left $350,000 for a match race between Ruffian and Foolish Pleasure, a 1 1/4 mile event. The race would be called "Great Match Race Stakes," Belmont Park.

On June 13, 1975 Jack Dreyfuss and Dinny Phipps, representing the NYRA made the official announcement. The race would be run July 6, 1975.

Ruffian, the big black filly, a product of Claiborne Farm, Bourbon County Kentucky and the Florida Bred colt Foolish Pleasure would engage in what was hailed as "The Battle of the Sexes.' As plans for the race began to develop, it was obvious to many that the NYRA saw the filly as the centerpiece of the race. As good as Foolish Pleasure was, it was not his presence that had generated the intense media coverage of the event. It was to be televised on CBS to some 18-20 million viewers.

It was not Foolish Pleasure's participation that had lent the match its timely social overtones. And it was not Foolish Pleasure whose symbolic importance had transcended the world of racing and sports in general. It was the larger than life filly with the perfect record: the coal black daughter of Reviewer and Shenanigans, the beauty, the speedball, the female , the freak.

The participants were scheduled for weighing in on June 25, 1975. NYRA press aides and officials mingled with a group of turf writers who had come to witness the event. The horses were being treated as if they were contenders for the heavyweight crown. As Ruffian gazed calmly at the crowd, the needle on the scale pointed to 1125 pounds.

Frank Morris, the Derby winner's groom led his horse to the scales. The scale registered 1061 pounds. Some people seeing the weight differential debated the significance of this. Foolish Pleasure kicked his hind legs into the air, scattering the crowd. The colt's exuberance caused some tense moments for the NYRA officials. If Foolish Pleasure sustained even the slightest injury before the race, the deal would be off. That would be a disaster.

The scheduled match race soon began to draw a great deal of national attention. The sport was enjoying this part, as only the Triple Crown could match what was happening. It was especially good for New York, still feeling the impact of the State Lottery, introduced in 1969. Off track betting followed in 1971. The race was a dream come true.

The jockeys for the race had yet to be announced. Jacinto Vasquez, the jockey on Foolish Pleasure's Derby win had also worked for Frank Whiteley, Ruffian's trainer. He had ridden both horses, which presented for him the need to make a decision. He decided to stay with the filly for the match race. He also continued to exercise Foolish Pleasure in his morning workouts. This led to some controversy, but LeRoy Jolley assured everyone he was comfortable and that he had no reason to be concerned.

Braulio Baeza was selected by LeRoy Jolley to ride his entry in the match race. The publicity for the upcoming event continued, as both Baeza and Vasquez were invited to appear on the "Tonight Show." As they were both contending for New York riding honors, the invitation was turned down by both.

There was a great deal of local media coverage, in particular for Jacinto Vasquez who was riding the filly. The city of New York passed out buttons that read —— "The Great Match," with a picture of the filly or the colt.

The draw for post positions was held on Thursday morning. Tom Fitzgerald, representing the NYRA picked the numbers. Marked one and two, the horses would leave from third and fourth stalls of the starting gate. The Thursday workout was phenomenal for Foolish Pleasure, -56 2/5 for -five furlongs. Frank Whiteley said of Foolish Pleasure. "He's a fine colt who is as honest as they come. He's got all kinds of speed. LeRoy's done an excellent job of keeping him in good form.."

Jacinto Vasquez was troubled the morning of the race. He attributed it to stress, having to choose between the two biggest horses of his life, That afternoon the paddock area was mobbed with people. Far beyond the number a major stakes event would attract.

Members of the Jockey Club mingled together with politicians and NYRA officials. The huge press corps was there along with photographers and the CBS television crew.

Ruffian emerged on the track first. Foolish Pleasure then came out on the track, and the fans cheered both great horses. Both appeared calm. Foolish Pleasure and Ruffian paraded in front of the huge crowd. At that point the colt was 4-5 and the filly was 2-5. George Cassidy, with the help of his assistant starters loaded the horses in the gate.

As Cassidy pressed the starters gun, Ruffian twisted her head down and to the left. The gates flew open and the race had begun. Foolish Pleasure was a step in front. The two horses raced as one down the backstretch —— both burning up the track. A couple of times the horses brushed and bumped, but nothing serious and both horses stayed on stride.

Then, Ruffian stuck her nose in front going the first quarter in :22 1/5. The colt was glued to the filly for a period of time, then Ruffian began to draw away. She had the lead by a half a length. Both riders heard a noise, a quick bright sound, like the snapping of a twig. Suddenly, Foolish Pleasure was a length in front, then two — three — four.

The announcer, Dave Johnson called in disbelief, "Ruffian has broken down! Ruffian has broken down!" The track crowd of 50,000 and some 18 million fans watching it at home watched as the nightmare unfolded. Ruffian kept on running, she wanted to run. This was the race of her life. She raced on three legs for a time. Vasquez tried to stop her; finally he pulled the filly to a halt.

Foolish Pleasure circled the track on his own. He had to cross the finish line with rider to collect the $225,000 winners share. Baeza did not enjoy the trip. This was not the way he wanted to win. His horse had raced at a terrific clip, and the track was lightning fast. His time for the first three quarters was 1:08 3/5. To run that fast on his own steam was fantastic, a tribute in part to both animals.

For LeRoy Jolley it was the longest race of his career. Jolley felt Foolish Pleasure would have won. The better horse was once again only a matter of belief, just as it had been before the race. The match had proved nothing. The "winners circle" ceremony was the least popular that had ever taken place at Belmont. There was no dispute over the fact Foolish Pleasure had won the race. It was a hollow victory, for he had not beaten anyone.

And through no fault of his own, he had failed to answer any of the questions that had prompted the match in the first place. An all out effort to save Ruffian failed. She died, and was buried in the infield at Belmont Park. A sad day for two great horses.

Foolish Pleasure did not win again as a three year old. He lost a head decision to Wajima in the Governor's Cup, and finished fifth behind the same horse in the Marlboro. His victory in the Suburban Handicap as a four year old was a great one. He gritted his teeth and allowed none of the other horses to pass him, including the great horse, Forego. Foolish Pleasure also won the Donn Handicap at Gulfstream, with a tremendous stretch run.

The last race of his career was the Arlington Golden International at Arlington Park. John Greer never got to see this one, as his plane from Albany, New York was delayed by fog. Foolish Pleasure won easily. Due to an infection, it was decided to retire him, and he was shipped to Kentucky for a farewell gallop at Keeneland.

Foolish Pleasure won 16 of 26 races and earned $1,216,705. Syndication shares were priced at $125,000 each. Total syndication value was $4.5 million. By 1994 the winner of the 1975 Kentucky Derby had stood in Kentucky, California and Wyoming. At the Horseshoe Ranch in Sheraton, Wyoming, Foolish Pleasure continued to attract attention. Ron Vanderhoff, the owner had provided the horse his own Post Office Box, and his own stationery. On November 11, 1994 Foolish Pleasure died of a ruptured intestine. He was twenty-two. He had sired 37 stakes winners, with three champions to his credit.

Seattle Slew

Member - National Thoroughbred Racing Hall of Fame
Saratoga Springs, N.Y.

6. Seattle Slew

T he day was February 15, 1974; the place, Ben S. Castleman's "White Horse Acres," a horse farm on Newtown Pike in Lexington, Kentucky. Paul Mallory, the farm manager had witnessed the broodmare My Charmer wander off from the other broodmares, a clue that she was close to becoming a mother for the first time. It had been eleven months since My Charmer had met Bold Reasoning, a new sire at Claiborne Farm.

At 7 P.M. that evening, a baby colt was foaled. Paul's wife Christine had been a part of the arrival of so many newborn racehorses, she had lost count. She was always mindful, that perhaps she was witnessing the birth of a Derby winner. It had never happened. Until now! Christine, aware that this foal was a great grandson of Bold Ruler, the father of Secretariat, felt different about this birth.

The foal would be one of 29,000 Thoroughbreds foaled in North America that winter and spring, so the odds against him being a Derby winner were huge. By breeding standards, the mating of an unproven sire with an unproven dam was described more as a blind date. Bold Reasoning, a big and fast late developing colt was a grandson of Bold Ruler. He did not race until March of his three year old season, but won his first seven races. He was bothered with a recurring throat disorder and retired as a four year old —— total earnings, $189,564.

My Charmer raced at two and at three, winning six times—— total earnings, $34,133. By January 1, 1975, the Bold Reasoning colt, now a yearling weighed close to seven hundred pounds. Ben Castleman nominated him for the Keeneland Summer Sales, a blue chip auction rivaled only by the Fasig-Tipton Saratoga Sales. Both sales enjoyed a reputation for offering only fashionable merchandise.

Keeneland rejected the colt nominated by Castleman, claiming he wasn't an outstanding looking individual. In addition, his pedigree, showing an unproven sire and dam wasn't all that good. That left Fasig-Tipton of Kentucky, a bargain basement auction inaugurated in Lexington in 1974 by the New York based company, as the logical alternative.

And so the colt was listed in the catalogue as number 128,—— a dark bay or brown, from the first crop of Boldnesian's brilliant son, Bold Reasoning. LeRoy Jolley, considered by many to be an expert at finding a good bargain was one of many who looked at the colt on Friday, July 18, 1975. Like most of the others, Jolley failed to see anything in the colt that excited him, thus paid little attention to him.

The Fasig-Tipton sale, a one day event was divided into an afternoon session and an evening session. At the afternoon part of the sale, Dr. Jim Hill, a veterinarian from Garden City, Long Island and Mickey Taylor of White Swan, Washington had purchased a yearling for $9,700 and another for $8,000. That evening, Hill flew back to New York, but Taylor remained for the evening session. They bought another yearling for $9,200; their real interest was focused on number 128. Prior to Jim Hill boarding the plane, the two buyers had talked and established a ceiling bid of $22,000 for the colt.

The bidding for hip number 128 started at $3,000, then Ralph Retler, the auctioneer managed to raise it up to $15,000., only to fail to go to $18,000. The gavel came down at $17,500, the bid presented by Mickey Taylor. At the time of purchase, Taylor and Hill were operating under a rather loose form of arrangement, sealed by a handshake. Officially, the horse was owned by Wooden Horse Investments, and the principal name provided was Karen Taylor, the wife of Mickey, a former airline stewardess. Her father, Delmar Pearson and Mickey were the principal stockholders in Wooden Horse Investments.

It was after the Kentucky Derby win in May of 1977 that Dr. Hill and his wife Sally emerged as co-owners of the horse, to be known as Seattle Slew. Seattle was the area where Taylor hailed from, and Slew was for the swampy alligator filled sloughs or "slews" in south Florida, the region where Hill had grown up. A total of thirteen yearlings were purchased by Wooden Horse Investments, Inc. that July day. Of the thirteen, nine were shipped to California and four (including number 128) stayed in the east. The Bold Reasoning colt was shipped to a farm in Maryland, where Paula Turner took on the role of schooling the young animal. The unofficial name for the colt at this time was "Baby Huey", after the overgrown duck in the cartoon strip. Paula was married to Billy Turner, a former steeplechase rider who was training Taylor's horses.

Billy Turner grew up around horses in southern Pennsylvania. At seventeen, he entered Emory College in Atlanta, spending weekends riding steeplechasers for W. Burling (Burley) Cocks. At that time he was 5 feet five inches tall and weighed 105 pounds. He soon grew to six feet two inches tall, thus abandoning the saddle to become a trainer of Thoroughbreds. By 1976 he had ten years of experience as a head trainer. In February of 1976, Paula Turner shipped the colt, now known as Seattle Slew to Belmont Park. Mike Kennedy, an exercise rider and friend of Billy Turner was on hand to greet the new arrival. He was not impressed with the rather common looking horse as he stood in the stall.

One morning in April, Turner told Kennedy to breeze the colt three-eighths of a mile; to be the first time under saddle. To help in the transition, a seasoned older stablemate would run with him. At a point in the run Kennedy put the reins together, chirped for speed —— and, "Wow!" The horse just ran, acting like he did not want to stop. This was one fast animal.

From that morning in April until June, Turner's horse was never asked for speed. He was just allowed to gallop easily, a mile or two a day, growing and muscling out and not hurting himself. Turner had a reason for this. He knew he had an exceptional horse. The horse was then shipped to Saratoga..

It wasn't long before the word around the Saratoga track was that Billy Turner had a Bold Reasoning colt that could fly. Turner made light of some of the conversations, but deep down knew he had a horse that was destined for stardom.

Seattle Slew never raced at Saratoga. He had injured his leg in the stall, delaying his debut as a two year old until he was back at Belmont. He made his debut on September 20,1976. The information in the "Daily Racing Form" that day was very brief, listing only three ordinary workouts for Slew. A workout on August 11, 1976 at Saratoga was listed incorrectly at 1:00 2/5 instead of 58 2/5. In fact it was cred-ited to Seattle Sue at 1:02. A time of 1:10 1/5 for six furlongs was not mentioned. Too bad.

The morning line on Seattle Slew was 10-1. At the completion of the fourth race, the opening odds for the fifth race appeared, show-ing Seattle Slew, the number eight horse at 7-5. Turner's horse was eighth in a twelve horse field. By the time they left the gate, the odds on Slew were 5-2. He won easily, going the six furlongs in 1:10 1/5 to equal the work out time at the Spa. Almost from the start of his racing career, there were people interested in buying him. In the first week of October 1976 Billy Turner entered Seattle Slew in a seven furlong al-lowance, which he won. This was followed by a win in the $137,000. Champagne Stakes on October 16th. Now he was referred to as the two year old American champion.

The owners elected to not race the champion again until the following year as a three year old. Seattle Slew was awarded an "Eclipse Award" with only three races to his credit. This caused some unrest with other handlers of two year olds, some with nine or ten races. The fact was that none of the other two year old candidates showed the promise that the Turner trained horse did.

By Derby day, May 7, 1977 Seattle Slew had raced to six straight victories, all with ease. He was a strong favorite to win the 103rd run for the roses. And he did! The local newspapers carried stories about Slew that Saturday morning. In Lexington, the birthplace of the favorite, once described as "ugly," the headlines in the "Hearld and Leader" read, "It's Slew's Day." The Louisville "Courier - Journal" headlines —— "Can He or Can't He? Slew Will Say Today."

For sure the skeptics were suggesting that Slew lacked the stamina to go the mile and a quarter this particular day. Billy Turner was subject to a great deal of criticism regarding his conservative approach to training the top three year old. His critics were claiming he should have trained his horse harder for such a test as the Derby. With Jean Cruget in the saddle Seattle Slew overcame a bumpy departure from the gate, then was rushed into contention. He duelled with LeRoy Jolley's horse For The Moment for the lead, and then with about a quarter of a mile left, put all the field away for a victory. Run Dusty Run was second followed by Sanhedrin in third. Jolley's horse fell back to finish eighth.

It was on to the Preakness. The skeptics were remaining skeptical, one in particular, Smiley Adams, the trainer of Run Dusty Run. Earlier he had claimed that Seattle Slew could be beat. He was now saying, "He's a nice colt, but he won't win the Triple Crown." He was wrong.

The Preakness was an easier ride for Cruget and Slew, in part due to the shorter distance and the ability of the three year old to display an early burst of speed. The other speedball entry, Cormorant took the early lead only to be worn down by Seattle Slew. Turner's horse went on to win by 1 1/2 lengths over Iron Constitution and the horse trained by Adams, Run Dusty Run. Seattle Slew had now started eight races and had won all eight. Not bad!

It was on to the Belmont. On June 11, 1977, with a muddy track underfoot, Seattle Slew would become the first undefeated Triple Crown Winner. Many great Derby winners have failed to repeat in the Preakness. Many that have went on to lose in the final event, the Belmont. The success of this horse, once described as "ugly and awkward" provided the sport of Thoroughbred Racing another "first." It was off to Esposito's for a celebration.

Seattle Slew had become the tenth three year old in Thoroughbred racing history to win the Triple Crown. The first, Sir Barton did it in 1919 and the last one to do it was Affirmed in 1978.

When it was all over, representatives from tracks all over the United States approached the owners of the great horse, trying to convince them to continue racing him. A decision was made to ship Seattle Slew to California in late June to race in the Swaps Stakes, an event for three year olds. The race also attracted J. O. Tobin, champion two year old in England, and a fifth place finisher in the Preakness behind Seattle Slew.

Once Turner's horse had arrived in California, he was the subject of a lot of publicity. This included a series of advertisements for "Xerox" Corporation. At this point the champion was not getting enough rest, which was evident on July 3, 1977. He finished fourth, running very poorly.

J. O. Tobin went on to victory. A decision was made to bring Slew back to New York, and ready him for the major fall races, skipping the historic Travers at Saratoga. As it turned out, Slew returned to the track the following year, as a four year old. Prior to his return to racing he was voted horse of the year over Forego, the top older horse and Affirmed, the two year old, who was then being heralded as the next Triple Crown winner. J. O. Tobin did not draw many votes, as beyond his victory in the Swaps, his overall record as a three year old was not impressive. As a four year old Seattle Slew suffered his second defeat, losing to Dr. Patches in the Patterson Handicap at the Meadowlands.

In late 1978 Seattle Slew was entered in the Marlboro but not as the favorite. The favorite was Affirmed, the latest Triple Crown winner. Slew's owners made a decision to put Angel Cordero, Jr. in the saddle. As the horses left the gate, Seattle Slew quickly took the lead and in a very relaxed fashion won by a three length margin over Affirmed. The critics were silenced, as Seattle Slew was again considered to be a valuable horse. Toward the end of 1978 Seattle Slew was shipped to Spendthrift Farm to begin a career as a stallion. In 1981 seven yearlings from Seattle Slew's first crop went through the Keeneland auction.

The price range for this first crop was from $75,000 to $700,000 for an average of $380,000. In 1982 there were fourteen yearlings from his second crop, auctioned at Keeneland and Saratoga. The average price that year was $554,643. This was about 50% higher than the previous year. The third crop of Seattle Slew yearlings were sold at an average price of $624,333, with three of them topping out in excess of $1 million. That same year, Secretariat yearlings averaged $296,692. Seattle Slew's record as a sire was an impressive one; by 1984 the average price of his yearlings was $1.316 million.

As of this writing, Seattle Slew is standing at Three Chimneys Farm in Midway, Kentucky.

Spectacular Bid

Member - National Thoroughbred Racing Hall of Fame
Saratoga Springs, N.Y.

7.   Spectacular Bid

I reflect on the fact, that as humans, we must learn to handle the many challenges that we are faced with, and find ways to work through the various stages of life. I believe this is also true of a Thoroughbred race horse. It is expected that they will learn to deal with many challenges, and be successful in many, perhaps all stages of life. As I wrote about Foolish Pleasure, I could not help but reflect on seeing him as an untried yearling parading around the auction ring that August night back in 1973. In the case of Seattle Slew, I never saw him as a yearling, but do remember seeing him as a four-year old, working out at Saratoga. As I now move on to my next selection, Spectacular Bid, I reflect on seeing him as a twenty-one year old stallion, petting his nose, only to be reminded that he still bites.

Fortunately, TV allowed me to see all three of them race to victory during their careers.

In 1976 the mare Spectacular was sent to Buck Pond Farm in Kentucky to be bred to Bold Bidder. In time she would produce her first foal, and he would be named Spectacular Bid.

And, like the subjects of the previous two chapters, when it came time for him to be brought to auction, it became a hard sell. As a yearling he had been entered in the Keeneland select summer sale, but was rejected.

He later sold at the Keeneland fall sale for $37,000. At that point he was shipped to the Middleburg, Virginia Training Center, to begin his schooling under the supervision of Barbara Graham and Buddy Delp.

In 1970 Grover G. (Buddy) Delp began an association with Robert and Harry Meyerhoff, the owners of Spectacular Bid. The Meyerhoff's were successful real estate developers in the Baltimore area. Delp, born in Harford County Maryland was introduced to the sport of racing by his stepfather, Raymond Archer. Archer had trained stakes winner Cape Cod.

A November 20, 1978 article that appeared in The Blood-Horse magazine quoted Delp as saying, "I've gotten a reputation as a trainer of claimers. I think I could do just as well with a class horse, if I had one." Well, in 1978 Delp had a colt with as much class as anyone could hope for. Barbara Graham had previously considered Spectacular Bid the best looking yearling she had ever seen.

As a two year old his first race was at Pimlico on June 30th. He beat Strike Your Colors, the son of Hoist The Flag. He raced again on July 22nd., finishing first, some eight lengths in front of Silent Native. In the August 2nd. Tyro Stakes at Monmouth, he finished fourth.

The 1978 Champagne Stakes brought a field of six to the starting gate. The favorites were General Assembly, the son of Secretariat, Tim The Tiger and Spectacular Bid, with Breezing On receiving some attention from the crowd.

As the race began, Breezing On went to the front. Spectacular Bid broke slowly. As they headed into the stretch, General Assembly and Tim The Tiger were the contenders. All of a sudden Spectacular Bid pulled away, opening up a four length lead. He went on to win by 2 3/4 lengths. As a two year-old, Spectacular Bid won five stakes races, establishing his credentials as the champion two year-old. His victories included the Champagne Stakes, Laurel Futurity and the Heritage Stakes. There was a great deal of excitement in the Delp stable as 1979 drew near. They were dealing with a soon to be three year-old with great potential.

And coming off two great years of racing with successive Triple Crown winners, Seattle Slew and Affirmed, the question was —— would their horse be next? Without a doubt 1978 had been one of the most exciting ever for the sport, with two superstars, Affirmed and Alydar. Tough act to follow.

By the spring of 1979, Spectacular Bid was beginning to really blossom as a three year old, with victories in the Florida Derby, Flamingo and the Blue Grass Stakes at Keeneland. It was on to the Kentucky Derby. The day was May 5, 1979. The Derby had been touted as a contest between Flying Paster and Spectacular Bid, two highly regarded horses with several wins to their credit.

Ron Franklin, the teenage jockey was picked by Buddy Delp to handle his colt. There were Delp critics that questioned the young riders ability to handle the pressure. As the gates opened for the 105th running of the Derby, Spectacular Bid stalled, causing a reaction from the crowd, in preparation for blaming the young rider. The Louisville area had been deluged with rain two days earlier, and the horses, in dealing with the packed mud, found the going difficult.

Flying Paster, the crowd's second choice scrambled, and third choice, Screen King seemed to jump up and down as Franklin took his big roan colt wide around the pack, sailing home for the victory. The win was number eleven for the horse, without a defeat. As a result of the win, Buddy Delp elected to go with his young jockey in the Preakness at Pimlico, Franklin's home track.

Spectacular Bid went on to win the Preakness. People continued to try and convince Delp to take his jockey off Spectacular Bid, despite his two victories in the Triple Crown events. Ron Franklin would ride the Bold Bidder colt in the Belmont. The morning of the race, Moe Hall, the groom discovered a pin in the horse's left front hoof. Following an examination of the hoof, a decision was made to allow the colt to race. The following day, Spectacular Bid was lame.

In the race, with Ron Franklin up, Spectacular Bid went straight to the front, almost as if it was a "mandate" that he establish a record. William Haggin Perry's Coastal, who had campaigned lightly and probably saved for this occasion, wore down the Derby winner and won.

The hoof injury caused Spectacular Bid to miss Saratoga's Jim Dandy and Travers Stakes. His next outing was August 26th at Delaware Park. Bill Shoemaker, replacing Ron Franklin rode the colt to a track record of 1:41 3/5, recording a seventeen length victory in the mile and a-sixteenth event. On September 8th. Spectacular Bid was matched against Coastal and General Assembly in the $300,000 Marlboro Cup at Belmont. General Assembly was fresh off a win in the Travers.

The Derby and Preakness winner finished five lengths in front of General Assembly, with Coastal in third place. His time of 1:46 3/5 was just shy of Secretariat's record time for the event. On October 6th. Spectacular Bid lost by 3/4 of a length to Affirmed in the Jockey Gold Cup. Coastal was third. In the Meadowlands Cup Handicap, once again racing against Affirmed, Spectacular Bid won with a time of 2:01 1/5. It was a three length victory over the second place horse, Smarten. The year 1979 was great for the people closest to Spectacular Bid. Mrs. Madelyn Jason, the breeder of the colt commented after his victory in the Derby, that her late father, William G. Gillmore would have been proud. "He was like any other man who races Thoroughbreds. He dreamed of coming here with a good horse. He was always one for doing things right."

In December, Spectacular Bid was shipped to Arcadia, California for the winter meeting. And then on to 1980, as a four year old. That year he had nine starts and won all nine. Among his wins were, The Charles H. Straub Stakes, Santa Anita Handicap, California Stakes, Armory L. Haskell Handicap and the Woodward, all Grade 1 events.

Spectacular Bid, undefeated in nine races at four was honored as America's overall champion for 1980. He won the Eclipse Award for Horse of The Year and for best older male. The award was presented in Los Angeles, California on January 23, 1981.

The $37,000 purchase at the 1977 Keeneland fall sale won 26 of 30 races for total earnings of $2.8 million. He was syndicated in 1980 for $22 million. In 1991, the champion was moved from Claiborne Farm in Kentucky to the Milfer Farm in Unadilla, New York.

Northern Dancer

Member - National Thoroughbred Racing Hall of Fame
Saratoga Springs, N.Y.

8. Northern Dancer

$\mathbf{F}$oolish Pleasure, Seattle Slew and Spectacular Bid, all bargain yearlings that went on to fame and fortune. As to Northern Dancer, it is also true. The difference is that as a yearling, Northern Dancer went unsold. At the 1962 Windfields yearling sale he failed to attract the $25,000. reserve and was returned to his owner, E.P. Taylor.

From that point Northern Dancer advanced to a great career on the track, followed by an even greater career as a stallion. In fact he became the most important breeding sire in the history of Thoroughbred racing. His life began on May 27, 1961 at National Stud Farm, Oshawa, Ontario, Canada. The colt, by Nearctic, out of Natalma had arrived. He would be named Northern Dancer. I learned from my research that Mr. Taylor's wife, Winifred had come up with the name for the colt.

Mrs. Taylor enjoyed picking names for the newborn foals. She would submit three names, in order of preference for each horse to the Jockey Club for approval. Andre Blaettler, yearling manager for Windfields Farm described the colt as a "real devil," due to the way he would fly around the paddock with a choppy gait, then skid to a halt at the gate. He was difficult to handle. In the early days, many Canadian Thoroughbred people paid little attention to Northern Dancer. Blaettler was not impressed with his looks at all.

On September 16, 1962, Northern Dancer was readied for the ninth annual sale of Windfields yearlings. Mr. Taylor assigned a reserve figure for all his yearlings. Taylor and his racing manager Joe Thomas established a value of $25,000 for the Nearctic colt. In all, forty eight yearlings were scheduled for the auction; Northern Dancer was the shortest. He measured fourteen hands, two and one half inches high. He tipped the scale at 955 pounds, some forty pounds below the average weight, Some people felt he looked more like a Quarter Horse than a Thoroughbred.

Windfields sold fifteen yearlings that day; the remaining thirty three (including Northern Dancer) went on to race for Mr. Taylor. As mentioned in chapter four, picking a winner from a herd of Thorough-bred yearlings is difficult. The bloodline and conformation is important, but not as important as the animal's "will to win." This part does not appear in the catalogue. Northern Dancer's pedigree was impressive, but both parents had been erratic.

Some two weeks after the yearling sale, the unsold were loaded in a horse van. They were transported to the Windfields training division across York Mills Road, a major thoroughfare that ran through the farm. It was time for school to begin. Northern Dancer was a difficult horse to handle. The first time an exercise rider mounted him, he was thrown into the air, then crashed to the ground. Riding Northern Dancer was like sitting on a powder keg, just waiting to explode.

In March of 1963, the two year old son of Nearctic was shipped to Woodbine Racetrack, Toronto. The track was located close to Windfields, about a half hour trip for the van. Horatio Luro was selected to train Northern Dancer. In addition, he would handle several of the other yearlings that had not been selected at the September sale. Peaches Flemming, an assistant to Luro was assigned to work with Luro's Canadian horses.

Northern Dancer's training was impeded by a recurring cracked heel, a form of psoriasis in the hollow at the back of the pastern (the short bone just above the hoof). This condition was carefully monitored by Flemming, out of fear of further irritation and possibility of ending up with a lame horse. On June 8, 1963 Northern Dancer ran his first official workout —— going three furlongs in :39.8, a very respectable time on a slow track. A month later, under rider Ramon Hernandez, the colt went three furlongs in thirty seven seconds, two seconds off the track record. On July 13, 1963 Northern Dancer was moved to Fort Erie for the summer meet, scheduled to begin in August.

On August 2, 1963 he was entered in a five and a half furlong maiden event for Canadian bred horses. As the official called for "riders up," Ron Turcotte, a young apprentice jockey was boosted onto the saddle. Turcotte, feeling he had something special in the colt, once beyond the 16th pole tapped the horse lightly. Northern Dancer exploded, opened up an eight length lead and held on to win.

Northern Dancer, in one short race had become "Windfields" best two year old and its best prospect for the Summer Stakes.

Northern Dancer was entered in the August 24th Woodbine's Summer Stakes event, a mile on the turf. He won, despite a very tough ride for Paul Bohenko, the jockey, as the horse came close to going down a couple of times, but held on to win.

It was evident that this was a good horse. He raced again on September 28, 1963 in the Cup and Saucer Stakes. This was a mile and one sixteenth over the turf; restricted to horses foaled in Canada. Northern Dancer shot out of the gate at Woodbine, took an early lead, but close to the wire he tired and was beaten by three quarters of a length by Grand Carcon, a longshot. The winner was one of the fifteen yearlings sold at Winfields in 1962, a bargain at $10,000. Interesting! The fifty - first running of the Coronation Futurity, the richest purse for two year olds was run on October 12, 1963. There were fifteen horses entered, including Northern Dancer, and Grand Carcon.

At the halfway point, Northern Dancer, with Ron Turcotte up was in control of the race. He won by six and a quarter lengths; Grand Carcon finished well back in Fifth place. Following that impressive victory, Windfields management decided to test the colt in the United States. Northern Dancer's first run on American soil would be November 27, 1963 in the Remsen at Aqueduct Race Track.

With Manuel Ycaza up Northern Dancer raced to an early lead in the first furlong of the Remsen, and went on to win the mile long event by an easy two lengths. During the race, the two year old injured the cracked heel once again; as a result he was brought back to

Windfields for a lengthy vacation. It was time for a major decision regarding Northern Dancer's upcoming career as a three year old.

Horatio Luro approached Mr. Taylor, informing him of a California based blacksmith who had experimented with a vulcanized patch on a winning Standardbred colt, Adios Jr. The trotter had a crack, very similar to the crack in Northern Dancer's hoof. Mr. Taylor agreed to bringing in Bill Dane, the blacksmith to examine the possibility of trying the patch on Northern Dancer. The big question was, would the colt go for it?

On December 9, 1963 at Belmont Park, Bill Bane worked for six hours preparing the patch of rubberized material that would bond the crack, yet be flexible enough to feel natural. The test would come when he would apply the patch to the horse's hoof. How would he react? As it turned out, Northern Dancer, munching on carrots during the application process never offered any resistance at all. The patch hardened quickly; the following week they walked him and then resumed his training.

Northern Dancer was shipped from Belmont to Hialeah Park in Miami, Florida during the week of Christmas. His return to training began with a very conservative approach, to allow him to regain strength. In time, as his pain eased the colt began to show strenth and enthusiasm.

Northern Dancer's handlers were confident at this point that he would be entered in the Derby, but did not feel that he could win. In January of 1964, he was nominated to the Triple Crown races. It was time to select a permanent jockey to handle the three year old contender. Up to this point, four jockeys had been aboard Northern Dancer at one time or another. Horatio Luro hired Bill Shoemaker, North America's leading jockey for seven years straight to be his rider.

Shoemaker had won the Derby in 1955 with Swaps, and again four years later aboard Tommy Lee. He agreed to ride the colt in the prep races, but would not commit for the Triple Crown events. The first scheduled prep race for Northern Dancer was the Flamingo, a mile and one eighth race at Hialeah on March 3rd. Prior to that he was entered in a six-furlong race on February 10, 1964. As Bill Shoemaker was not available, Luro hired Bobby Ussery to ride the colt. Ussery would become the fifth jockey to ride Northern Dancer.

This race turned out to be a rough outing for both the horse and rider. The son of Nearctic left the gate real fast, only to be bumped and knocked off stride, falling to the rear of the pack. He came on to be third behind Chieftan and Mom's Request. Luro was very upset with Ussery's handling of the horse and denounced him publicly for giving the three year old a bad ride.

The hopes of getting Northern Dancer to the Kentucky Derby was now in doubt. The days that followed were filled with a lot of tense moments. In part, due to the fact Ussery had used a strong whip on the horse there was fear that Northern Dancer would react to the distractions the next time out. A large crowd, the walking ring, starting gate, or the race itself might trigger an association with Ussery's whip. The owner, knowing Bill Shoemaker was the best rider at the time, with ability to communicate with horses elected to go in the Flamingo.

Northern Dancer won the Flamingo by two lengths over Mr. Brick. Quadrangle was third, some ten lengths back. The colt was then moved to Gulfstream Park in North Miami to prepare for the April 4th. Florida Derby. In the Florida Derby, with Bill Shoemaker up, Northern Dancer left the gate in a flash, and then was forced to run close to the rail and bide his time. By the final turn, the horses that had passed Northern Dancer started to fade. Northern Dancer went on to win by a length over The Scoundrel. The time for the race was 1:50.8, for a mile and one eighth. Northern Dancer was headed for the Kentucky Derby.

On April 10, 1964, Northern Dancer arrived at Keeneland Racetrack in Lexington. It was the end of a 1200 mile trip from Gulfstream. The van and crew delivering the colt had rested for a few days at a farm in Georgia owned by Horatio Luro.

The Blue Grass Stakes, the featured event of Keeneland's spring meet and a Derby prep race was going to be run April 23rd. It had been announced that Bill Shoemaker had now decided to ride Hill Rise in the Derby instead of Northern Dancer. Hill Rise was an outstanding three year old that had campaigned in California. Shoemaker was convinced that Hill Rise was the better horse. He was wrong.

Horatio Luro hired Bill Hartack to ride Northern Dancer. Hartack had won his third Derby in 1962 aboard Decidedly. He agreed to ride Luro's colt in the Blue Grass Stakes.

At the start of the Blue Grass, Northern Dancer bolted out of the gate, taking an early lead. Hartack then held his horse back, and Royal Shuck went to the front. In the stretch, Northern Dancer coasted into the lead. Allen Adair, a Kentucky bred came charging out of the pack; Hartack, seeing the oncoming horse over his shoulder, loosened his grip, and with that, Northern Dancer finished a half a length in front of the fast moving Allen Adair. Hartack, rather than pulling his horse up, took him an extra furlong —— to a distance of a mile and a quarter. His time was 2:03. Hartack's win in the 1962 Derby was recorded as 2:00.4. The thought was that Northern Dancer might not be the best bet to win the Derby.

On April 25, 1964 Northern Dancer was moved from Keeneland to Churchill Downs in Louisville, Kentucky, some seventy miles away. The Kentucky Derby is viewed by prominent horse people and turf writers, as well as a lot of plain folks as the greatest horse race in North America. It was now May 2nd —— Derby Day. The time had arrived for E. P. Taylor's little three year old horse to tackle the first leg of the Triple Crown.

The excitement surrounding the Derby is like the excitement that surrounds golf's master's tournament every April. As Northern Dancer was readied for the event, he was quite jumpy. Finally, the bugler sounded the call to the post and the band played the "Star Spangled Banner." Then came "My Old Kentucky Home," and over 100,000 fans began to sing. Northern Dancer joined the action by bucking, then calmed down as he entered the track area. He reacted to the initial attempt to move him into the starting stall, then when he was ready, he eased into his designated spot.

They're off! The field was charging down the track. At the first turn, Northern Dancer was on the rail, sitting seventh. Coming off the backstretch, he was still on the rail, trapped by other horses. He had caught up with the front runners, but had no place to go. Then the colt shot sideways, right in front of Hill Rise, moving around the leaders. Northern Dancer, some four inches shorter than most of the other horses took Hill Rise right up to the wire, stretched his neck to win by a "neck."

The time for the race was two minutes flat, a new track record. It was on to the Preakness. Northern Dancer won the Preakness. The Scoundrel was second, by a head over Hill Rise. Wow! It was now on to the Belmont. He lost the Belmont, finishing third behind horses he had previously beat. Northern Dancer's next scheduled race was the 105th running of the Queen's Plate on June 20th. There was concern over a tendon injury sustained in the Belmont. He won the event by seven and a half lengths in front of Langcrest. It was to be his last race. Northern Dancer would be prepared for a new career, to begin in the fall.

I mentioned earlier in the writing that the breeding business carries a great deal of risk. The fact that Northern Dancer failed to win the mile and a half Belmont Stakes led many horse people to believe that his foals would be good sprinters, but not distance horses. The experts were as skeptical of his potential as a stallion, as they had been about his potential as a racehorse.

Officially, Northern Dancer was retired on November 6, 1964. Beginning in 1965 E. P. Taylor's great horse would be available for stallion duties for a fee of $10,000. It did not take long for Northern Dancer's book to fill up. There were offers for a syndication, but Mr. Taylor refused them. Mares were shipped from some of America's top farms, including Claiborne Farm, Spendthrift and Greentree Stud in Kentucky. They also came from Maryland, Pennsylvania and Virginia. Business was good!

Northern Dancer's potential as a stallion was evident right from the start, as from his first crop came three champions. That first year, seven Northern Dancer yearlings sold at Keeneland and Saratoga. All seven were winners. In 1968, his fourth year as a stallion, E. P. Taylor elected to move his prize stallion to the Maryland Division of Windfields Farm. He arrived in Maryland on December 3rd. The great son of Nearctic sired 635 foals over twenty - three seasons. Of his 146 stakes winners, twenty - six were declared champion in Ireland, England, France, Italy, the United States and Canada.

The first Northern Dancer descendant to win the Kentucky Derby was Ferdinand, son of Nijinsky II. The Minstrel, a 1974 foal was horse of the year in England and Ireland in 1977. I mentioned in Chapter four the $13.1 million record sale in the Keeneland 1985 July sale. That colt was a grandson of Northern Dancer.

On November 16, 1990 in Chesapeake Bay, Maryland, Northern Dancer was being treated for Colic. He was in a tremendous amount of pain, and his handlers were very concerned because of an existing heart condition. Alan McCarthy, the veterinarian met with Charles Taylor, the son of the late E. P. Taylor. Charles Taylor had been in charge of the business since his father's death in 1989. It was decided that it was not fair to let the horse suffer.

Northern Dancer was put to sleep at 6:15 A.M. In Canada his passing was treated by the media like that of a popular head of state. A great hero was gone.

9.   And Others

My original idea for this book was to write about Saratoga, with a great deal of emphasis on the impact the city has had on Thoroughbred racing.   In addition, I wanted to write about some bargain yearlings that became champions.

As mentioned in the preface, my visit to Lexington in 1995 led me to a decision to do the book differently.   I did, however stay with the idea to write about the bargain yearlings.   In addition to my four main choices, I wanted to write about others that would fit the theme for this part of my book.   My selections were made after a great deal of deliberation, searching for horses I believed would compliment the four of them.   I continue by offering a commentary, written in "random" fashion on some damn good horses.

Morello, an 1890 foal by Eolus, out of Cerise brought a price of $100., as a yearling.   Of course, back then if a horse got to the races, the purses were between $400. to $1,000.   As a two-year old, Morello won the Belmont Futurity and the Sea and Sound Stakes, cosponsored by the Coney Island and New York Jockey Clubs.

As a three-year old he won the Drexel Stakes Sweepstakes, an event for foals of 1890.   I wonder what the feed bill was back then.   If we look in the record books, it will list Pensive as the winner of the 1944 Kentucky Derby and Preakness.   The records also show that Pensive would never win again, but another 1941 foal, one by Equestrian would win 25 stakes events following his sixth place finish in the 1944 Preakness. Stymie was foaled at King Ranch on April 4, 1941, a chestnut colt out of

Stop Watch. A tough ordinary looking chestnut foal with a blaze face and a tendency to run with his head held high.

He was claimed for $1,500.00 by Hirsch Jacobs, and would become the first horse to win $800,000. He would also be the first to win $900,000. In the beginning, he went to the post 14 times before he won. As a two-year old Stymie had twenty-eight starts with four victories to his credit.

Stymie's first start as a three-year old was on January 1, 1944, when he finished second. He then raced in the Hialeagh Stakes, losing by two lengths. He also lost the next two outings, finishing third in the Flamingo and second in a division of the Wood Memorial. Both races were won by Greentree's Stir Up. Up to this point, Stymie had not shown any real potential.

At Pimlico he finished fourth to Gramps Image and Calumet Farm's Pensive in the Chesapeake Stakes. Pensive, as mentioned earlier had won both the Derby and Preakness; in both these events, Stymie was anything but impressive. He raced 57 times in his first two seasons, winning only seven times and $52,600.

Then, as a four-year old he was the second leading money winner, and voted champion handicapper. At five he finished in the money nineteen of his twenty starts. At that point his total earnings were up to $517,000., second only to Whirlaway, the 1941 Triple Crown winner. Some of his best races that year were the Grey Lag Handicap, the Whitney Stakes and the Saratoga Cup. He beat Assault by 2 1/2 lengths in the Gallant Fox, but lost to him in the Pimlico Special.

As a six-year old, Stymie grew his total earnings to $816,000. by year end. His greatest race was the International Gold Cup, racing against Natchez, Phalanx, Talon, Assault and Endeavour II. In that race Natchez went to the front, but nothing really happened, for at least a mile and a quarter. Then, Eddie Arcaro sent Assault after the leader, but he could not take Natchez. Stymie, coming on the outside was not to be denied as he caught Natchez to win by a neck, earning the money title.

As a seven-year-old, Stymie's total earnings reached $911,335. In the Monmouth he fractured his sesamoid and was retired. He was later brought back to race, but did not do well. His career earnings of $918,485. stood as a record until Citation became the first equine millionaire in 1950.

Stymie, as a stallion stood in Kentucky and California. His foals included eleven stakes winners, but none compared with Stymie. He died on June 24,1962 at the age of twenty-one. At the time of his death, he was standing at Hagyard Farm in Lexington.

If there was ever a natural to play the role of the ugly duckling, it had to be John Henry. He was a 1975 foal by Ole Bob Bowers, out of Once Double. His sire was described as an ill tempered animal, and together with the dam earned the label —a "very homely pair."

As a colt, John Henry was small and ugly, with a lousy disposition. In his yearling year, he was purchased at the Keeneland winter sale, kind of an equine fire sale. John Calloway, the purchaser paid $1,100. for the colt. He liked the dam side of the pedigree. In time Calloway became disenchanted with his horse and sent him back to Keeneland for resale. In 1977 John Henry was purchased a second time for $2,200. The new owner was Harold Snowden of Lexington, Kentucky.

Snowden, exercising a great deal of caution began training, which went fairly well. The horse broke easy, but was considered rough in the stall. On the track he was all business. At one point, Snowden made a decision to geld John Henry, to calm him down.

In time, Snowden elected to sell the horse to a Japanese agent, Akiko Mc Varish, but the sale was voided and John Henry was brought back to the farm. He was then bought by Colleen Madere, Dorthea Lingo and Dorthea's son John for a price of $10,000. In March of 1978, following a poor showing at the races, John Henry was returned to Harold Snowden in exchange for a couple of promising two-year olds. At that time, Snowden decided to sell his horse again. Sam Rubin, a laundry owner from New York City bought him for $25,000. It was a gamble, but it turned out to be the steal of the century. John Henry would go on to win 39 races, almost half of his 83 career starts. His career earnings were $6,597,947, surpassing such superstars as Spectacular Bid, Affirmed and Kelso.

Along the way, John Henry appeared at eighteen different tracks in the United States, and one in Japan. He carried seventeen different jockeys. In 1981, John Henry won the $1 million Arlington and won horse of the year honors. A comparison with other great geldings,

Kelso	(1960-1964)	$1,977,896
Forego	(1974-1976)	$1,938,957
John Henry	(1981-1984)	$6,597,947

It was thought John Henry would race as a ten-year old, but a strained ligament in his left foreleg would prevent this from happening. Sam Rubin, with an announcement at Hollywood Park in front of 40,000 fans stated, "The Time Has Come." John Henry, one of the great ones stepped down as a champion.

A June 7, 1979 article that appeared in a Lexington newspaper began with the following headline, "Exceller to Be Catalogue Cover Horse for July Keeneland Yearling Sale." Exceller, the all time leading money winning Thoroughbred purchased at Public auction will be the catalogue cover for Keeneland's July 23-24 selected yearling sale, so stated the opening paragraph.

Exceller was purchased in 1974 by Nelson Bunker Hunt, the industrialist, entrepreneur at the 1974 Keeneland summer sale for $25,000. The son of Vaguely Noble-Too Bald was sold by the Mrs. Charles W. Engelhard's consignment. His early days of racing were in Europe, where in four starts as a two-year old he won once.

At the start of his three-year old season it was assumed he was a bit below the standards of the major European classic hopefuls.By mid summer he was right up to their class. He won the Grand Prix de Paris, the Prix Royal-Oak and the Prix ru Lys. At four he won France's

Grand Prix-de Saint Cloud and England's Coronation Cup. He then returned to North America.

Exceller added the Canadian International Championship at Woodbine and took second in the Man o'War and third in the Washington, D.C. International. At five his big race was the Jockey Club Gold Cup, racing against a couple of good horses, Affirmed and Seattle Slew. In the early going, Affirmed and Life's Hope raced head and head with Seattle Slew.

Exceller was some 22 lengths back as the horses moved through the backstretch at Belmont. Suddenly, Slew put away Affirmed, as the 1978 Triple Crown winner went out of contention with a saddle problem. Seattle Slew continued to race hard, pulling away from Life's Hope to take the lead. But not for long. Exceller made up the entire 22 lengths as they positioned for the stretch run. At this point Slew was in a real battle with the Vaguely Noble colt.

Exceller, in front by a neck fought Seattle Slew off, crossing the finish line, winning by a nose. It was one of fifteen first place finishes for Exceller. He was bred to be good. Exceller was retired after suffering a small crack in his left front coffin bone during the running of the Century Handicap at Hollywood Park. His career earnings at that time were $1,654,002.

Canonero II, the 1971 Kentucky Derby winner was purchased in 1969 for $1,200. at the Keeneland Fall sale. He had a cracked right foreleg. A bay colt, the son of Prentendre, out of Dixieland II, his victory in the Derby was witnessed by 124,000 fans. Jim French was second, with Bold Reason placing third. Canonero II was on his way to the Preakness.

The second leg of the 1971 Triple Crown began with Canonero II rushing to the outside, challenging Eastern Fleet for the lead. The two horses battled head to head, some five lengths in front of the rest of the field, down the backstretch heading for the final turn. Gustavo Avila was into a strong gallop, taking the lead briefly. Canonero II, with a tremendous stretch run came on to win. The question at this point —— do we have a Triple Crown winner?

The Kentucky bred had surprised a lot of people when he won the Derby. Following that event there were reports that he would be sold after the running of the Belmont, or syndicated for about $4 million. In preparation for the Belmont, there was a great deal of anxiety surrounding the Juan Arias stable. As it turned out, history would once again repeat, as Canonero II was denied the Belmont and the Triple Crown. The champion performed well that day, but a quarter mile from the finish line a lanky bay by the name of Pass Catcher ran by the field to win. Canonero II finished fourth in the 1 1/2 mile final leg of the Triple Crown. Canonero II was syndicated for $1.6 million, and retired to Gainesway Farm in Kentucky.

Sunday Silence, a black colt bred by Oak Cliff Thoroughbreds was a 1986 foal. In the 1987 Keeneland sale, he was brought back for $17,000. and later sold privately. As a two year old, the son of Halo, out of Wishing Well started three times, winning once. He began his outstanding three-year old season early in 1989 with a California winning streak that included an 11 length victory in the Santa Anita Derby.

On the east coast all eyes were on Easy Goer, and as the Triple Crown events drew near both Sunday Silence and Easy Goer were being mentioned as favorites. The date was May 6, 1989 —— Derby Day. The temperature in Louisville that day was 43 degrees, coldest on record. The field had been reduced to fifteen, due to Notation being scratched.

The setting was set for the race. Easy Goer, with Pat Day seeking his sixth consecutive victory broke well, while Sunday Silence, with Pat Valenzuela up went off poorly. In the opening furlongs, the good horse, Houston took the lead. Sunday Silence stood in fourth, as Easy Goer was poised for a strike. Sunday Silence then went out, well in front of Easy Goer at the three-eighths pole. Easy Goer dropped back to seventh, then for a moment raced in eighth position.

Valenzuela called on his horse to react to an opportunity to overcome Houston and Northern Wolf. In the stretch, with Easy Goer still struggling, Sunday Silence swooped to the left when Valenzuela hit him on the right. He almost slammed into Northern Wolf, but the jockey righted him in time. He went on to win with the slowest Derby time in 31 years, 2:05.

The 1989 Preakness was the first one for jockey, Pat Valenzuela. His father, Ismael (Milo) Valenzuela had won the 1958 Preakness with Tim Tam and again in 1969 aboard Forward Pass. Sunday Silence won the Preakness, with Easy Goer a close second followed by Rock Point. It was an exciting race, with the Derby winner involved in two bumping incidents early in the race. First, by Northern Wolf and then by Pulverizing. He survived both incidents and continued, but dropped back, going down the backstretch.

As the horses began their stretch run, Easy Goer was very close to the rail, nearly brushing it, racing in what appeared to be synchronized stride with Sunday Silence. In the final yards, Pat Day turned Easy Goer's head slightly to the right, while Valenzuela switched his whip and slapped, Sunday Silence on the right. Sunday Silence won by a nose. Wow!

As of the 1989 Preakness, twenty-two horses had won the first two Triple Crown events, but only eleven had gone on to win the Belmont. Would Sunday Silence be the next Triple Crown winner? His time of 1:53 4/5 in the Preakness was two fifths of a second slower than Tank's Prospect's record time. Sunday Silence was prepared for the Belmont.

For three weeks Easy Goer had been to Sunday Silence as Sham had been to Secretariat and Alydar to Affirmed. In the final leg of the 1989 Triple Crown, Easy Goer would shed the cloak of runner up.

The Belmont got off to a good start, with smooth sailing, for both Sunday Silence and Easy Goer. At the start of the final quarter mile, the tension began to intensify as Pat Day sent Easy Goer to the outside. In the stretch, Day kept driving his horse, whipping him on the left, running away from Sunday Silence and the rest of the field. Sunday Silence fell victim to Easy Goer, finishing second by a length over LeVoyageur. In November, Sunday Silence and Easy Goer faced each other in the $3 million Breeders Cup Classic. Chris McCarron, elected to the Hall of Fame in 1989 was picked to ride Sunday Silence in place of the suspended Valenzuela.

As the horses left the gate in the event held at Gulfstream Park, McCarron's horse came away in good order, racing well out in the track. As they entered the far turn, Sunday Silence went after the leader, Blushing John. In the stretch run, Sunday Silence passed both Easy Goer and Blushing John to win by a neck in 2:001/5. A year earlier McCarron had won with Alysheba. As a four year old, Sunday Silence won the Californian, only to be forced into retirement shortly thereafter. He was sent to stud in Japan. His career earnings were $4,968,554.

Dennis Diaz grew up on his family's dairy farm in Tampa, Florida. After a few years in the insurance business, he ventured into the sport of Thoroughbred racing. The first couple of years were filled with a great deal of adventure, as he experienced up and down times. Then came —— Spend A Buck. The 1982 foal, sired by Buckaroo; the dam being Belle De Jour, would once again prove that good horses don't have to cost a lot of money. The question —— how do you know it will be a good horse?

Diaz, owner of Hunter Farm in Tampa purchased his good horse as a yearling for $12,500. He began racing him as a two-year old, winning $667,985, capturing the Arlington - Washington Futurity and finishing third in the Breeders' Cup Juvenile.

At three he really made an impact on the sport, by winning the Kentucky Derby, beating Stephan's Odyssey and Chief's Crown, two outstanding horses. Following the Derby, there were offers to purchase interests in the horse. Dennis Diaz and his trainer, Cam Cambolat discussed the possibility of racing the colt in the Preakness. There was a conflict, an opportunity to race in the Jersey Derby, a $600,000 event with a bonus of $2 million to the winner.

Spend A Buck was eligible for the Jersey Derby due to two previous wins at Garden State and his Kentucky Derby victory. The date for the race was May 27,1985 only nine days after the Preakness. It was strongly felt the horse could not run in both events. The experts were saying that if Spend A Buck were to win the Triple Crown, his value would be close to $40 million. This, of course was not a sure thing. The $2.6 million was not a sure thing either, but perhaps, almost a sure thing.

A decision was made that Spend A Buck would race in the Jersey Derby, and skip the remaining two Triple Crown races. Spend A Buck won the Jersey Derby by a neck over Brushwood Stables Creme Fraiche, qualifying for the biggest single day paycheck in racing history. The victory, with Laffit Pincay in the saddle increased the horse's total earnings to $3,998,509.

It proved to be an exciting race, right from the start as the winner stumbled at the gate, but recovered to set the pace, only to be pushed by HuddlerUp and Creme Fraiche. Creme Fraiche charged to the front on the swing into the stretch, rallying from sixth place. Spend A buck ran the last quarter in 27 3/5 and the final half time in :53 3/5, closing in 2:02 3/5, a great performance.

Spend A Buck retired to stud at Lane's End Farm in Versailles, Kentucky. His ten victories in fifteen starts earned him $4,220,689.; at that time placing him second to John Henry with respect to total earnings. As of this writing, the record for race earnings is held by Cigar, an amount just shy of $10 million.

I find it truly amazing, the amount of fun I have had in developing my original idea, and carrying it to fulfillment: the end result being the book you have just read. For me to explain in a few words how I feel about this book is not possible. Therefore, it will be more than just a few words. I wanted to do a book about Saratoga, and relate to some of my personal experiences. As to style, I have designed both my books with a great deal of similarity. And, with respect to the two books, people have asked; you are writing a history book? I reply with, "there is just enough history to keep it from being a history book." I will never consider myself a historian. In addition, I would never attempt to write an information type book, one dealing with technology or statistical data.

My style of writing, the blending of real life experiences with a touch of history offers me the opportunity to express myself with a great degree of sincerity. In this book I have been able to write about two popular American cities, linking them together with the Thoroughbred —— that breed of horse—— "bred from the best blood." This is, "as I see it."

Thank you.

Bibliograghy

Bradley, Hugh   Such Was Saratoga Doubleday: Doran
New York 1940

Finney, Humphrey S. (With Raleigh Burroughs) Fair Exchange New
York: Charles Scribner's Sons 1974

Crist, Steven   The Horse Traders: W.W. Norton & Co. New
York-London

Wharton, Mary E.   The Horse World of the Bluegrass:

Bowen, Edward L.   The John Bradford Press Lexington, Kentucky
1980

Cady, Steve   Seattle Slew: Penquin Books-The Viking
Press Silverman, Barton, New York, N.Y.
1977

Schwartz, Jane   Ruffian: Burning From The Start
Ballantine Books, New York

Ranck, George Washington History of Lexington: Robert Clarke &
Co. Cincinnati 1872

Staples, Charles Richard The History of Pioneer Lexington:
Transylvania Press, Lexington Ky.

Various Contributing Authors   The Treasury of Horses: Octopus
Books Limited, London - New York-
Sydney- Hong Kong

Lennox, Muriel   Northern Dancer -The Legend and His Legacy:
Beach House Books - A Division of
Lennox Group Communications Inc.
Toronto -Ontario, Canada

Coleman, J. Winston Jr.   Stage Coach Days: The University
Press of Kentucky

Additional References for Part II

Rudy, William H.   Racing In America 1960 - 1979

Private Printing   The Jockey Club -1980

Various Articles   The Blood-Horse Magazine, Property of
National Museum of RacingAnd Hall of Fame
Saratoga Springs, N.Y.